TRY GOD

Other books by Laura Hobe

THE MARRIAGE GAP
(with Dr. Stanley Rosner)

THE MEANING OF CHRISTMAS

THE MEANING OF LOVE

TAPESTRIES OF LIFE

TRY GOD

by LAURA HOBE

foreword by David Wilkerson

DOUBLEDAY & COMPANY, INC.
GARDEN CITY, NEW YORK
1977

TRY GOD is a registered trademark of Tiffany & Co.

Library of Congress Cataloging in Publication Data

Hobe, Laura.
Try God.

1. Converts–United States–Biography. 2. Walter Hoving Home. 3. Church work with delinquent girls–New York (State)–Garrison. I. Title.
BV4930.H6 248'.246 [B]
Library of Congress Catalog Card Number 76-50771
ISBN 0-385-12443-0

Printed in the United States of America
FIRST EDITION

To John

PREFACE

Some people say that human beings can't change; some say they can. I don't agree with either opinion. In this book about changed lives, it is Jesus Christ who makes the difference.

In Garrison, New York, there is a home for troubled girls. It is called The Walter Hoving Home, and it is affiliated with Teen Challenge, the nationwide ministry to youth founded by the Reverend David Wilkerson.

On Fifth Avenue in New York City there is a store whose name has become an American legend. It is called Tiffany & Co., and its chairman is Walter Hoving, a man known for his dedication to his Lord.

In all parts of this country there are girls in need of help. Some are alcoholics and drug addicts, some are thieves and cheats, some are runaways and prostitutes. They are at war with their families, with their society, and with themselves, and the last thing in the world they want to hear about is God. Yet they come to The Walter Hoving Home, usually after they have tried everything else and failed. Only then—and almost with defiance—are they ready to try God.

How all these seemingly unrelated elements fit together into a miracle is the story of TRY GOD.

The first time I went to the Home to talk to some of the girls, I met one who had arrived two days earlier. She had been a pill user and was terribly underweight. Her eyes were dull, and her skin was gray. She was restless and desperate for a cigarette, which she was not allowed to have. As we talked we had to keep moving from room to room, from chair to chair, because she could not sit still. She was so depressed that, frankly, I thought she wasn't going to make it. When she said she would write to me, I didn't take her seriously. But I prayed for her, and I prayed that she would stay. God would do the rest.

Two months later I got a letter from her. "I was just thinking of you and I thought I would drop a short note to let you know all is great," she wrote. "Praise God! I'm so happy in the Lord. Believe me, I've never been happier since I came to the Home, and for once in my life I believe with all my being that there is hope for me—and the credit all goes to Jesus Christ, because without him I'm nothing, with him I'm everything." Now, that's a miracle!

I welcome this opportunity to thank the people who helped me reach into the background for this story: Walter Hoving, chairman of Tiffany & Co., and Anne Balsan, his secretary; the Reverend John Benton, director of the Home, and his wife, Elsie; Joyce Dyrud and all the other members of the staff; Samantha Veit for typing the manuscript. I have a special kind of gratitude for the girls in The Walter Hoving Home and have changed their names and some of the details of their lives in an effort to protect their identities.

FOREWORD

This is the story of God's love reaching out to change lives—from the glitter of Tiffany's to the gutter of rebellion and addiction. Girls who have been given up by society become powerful missionaries and love-channels of God's mercy.

You will find it hard to read this book without being moved to tears in your realizing the power of Christ's love at work so drastically. What could it be but a miracle when a derelict girl, who is ashamed even to look at herself in a mirror, is so turned around through faith in Christ that she becomes a radiant witness and a beautiful lady?

And that is what this book is all about: miracles, changes, and tough love. The love John and Elsie Benton have shared with hopeless girls is not sentimental and idealistic. It is a tough love that balances discipline with compassion. Walter Hoving, chairman of Tiffany & Co., was sent by God to help lift the load that, at times, seemed almost crushing. How God brought all these people together is a miracle story, and you will not soon forget it. As you read, thank God that you and your family have been spared the agonies of those whose stories are being told.

I recommend TRY GOD because I know you will like it.

David Wilkerson

TRY GOD

CHAPTER 1

It was midnight and very cold and windy when Sandy finally arrived in Peekskill, New York, along with three young men whose names she never could remember. In fact, she couldn't remember how long she had known them, or if she had ever known them at all before that night. No matter. The drive from New York City was one she didn't want to make alone, so when she left the bar where she had been drinking since late afternoon she waved her arm, and anyone who followed was welcome. At least her three companions kept her awake with their jokes.

Awake. That was a joke in itself. Being awake was the worst part of her life, and she did everything she could to avoid it. But if she fell asleep at the wheel and went off the road into a ditch, she might never wake up, and she wasn't ready for that kind of sleep. Not yet.

When her car—a faded, much-dented Firebird that had been stolen and passed on to her for fifty dollars—abruptly stopped running, it seemed like one more joke to her. They were in the middle of the road outside a bar, the only sign of life she had seen as they approached the town. It was a one-story building made to look like a log cabin in front, and the red neon letters spelling BAR flickered nervously over the door. Somebody ought to change a bulb or something, Sandy thought, and then she giggled, deciding that she and the sign were two of a kind: burned out. Maybe somebody ought to replace her, too, and throw her away.

"What's so funny?" It was the short one, sitting behind her, the one with the quick answers. He leaned forward, resting his arms on the back of her seat.

Sandy shook her head and turned off the ignition. "I am," she said, realizing that he wouldn't understand.

"Who cares?" the thin blond man beside her said. "I got no complaints."

"I'm getting cold." The older, slightly more muscular man—probably the thin one's brother—put his hand on the floor near the heater, which of course had died with the engine. "Let's go inside."

When Sandy opened the car door and got out, the air was icy against her face. Any minute it was going to snow —one more joke. She wasn't dressed for the cold. She wore jeans, a light pink T-shirt, and a dark blue nylon windbreaker. Somewhere in her suitcase, which she thought she remembered putting in the trunk of the car, was a heavy sweater. She used to have a warm coat—tan, with a zip-out pile lining—until a few days ago. She didn't know where or how she lost it. One day, when she went to put it on, it wasn't there. Lots of her things went like that.

There were a few cars parked along a stockade fence next to the bar, which proved that she had been wrong about the residents of Peekskill. Not everyone turned out the lights and went to bed before midnight. *But I'll bet every mechanic in town is out cold,* she thought.

"You go ahead in," she said to the others. She had seen a telephone booth by the stockade fence. "I have to make a call."

Against the darkness of so many trees, the light inside the phone booth made her feel as if she were on a stage with all the world looking at her. She put in her dime and was about to dial the number when she hesitated. *Why not call collect?* she thought. It was only a local call, but why not hold onto her dime as long as she could? Pushing her dark curly hair away from her ear with the receiver, she dialed 0 for operator and then dialed the number.

Three rings—not much of a wait, considering the hour. "The Walter Hoving Home—hello." It was a woman, and her voice was young.

"This is a collect call to anyone who answers, from Sandy McKay," the operator said.

"I'm sorry," the young voice answered, "we cannot accept the charges. We'll be glad to speak to Sandy McKay if she wants to call us herself."

Sandy swore. With her left hand she dug into the pocketbook slung over her shoulder, trying to find her cigarettes. She really wanted to hang up, but out of pure stubbornness she held on.

"The party will not accept the charges," the operator began to repeat, but Sandy cut her off.

"I heard, I heard," she snapped. Oh, how she wanted a drink, right now!

"If you wish to make the call, please hang up and dial again," the operator said.

Sandy had found her cigarettes, which gave her courage. "Thanks for all your help," she said, and then slammed the receiver onto its cradle as hard as she could, hoping it knocked the operator's head off.

She pulled out a cigarette and found some matches in her windbreaker pocket to light it. As she inhaled, she shivered. The cold was getting to her. Still, she wasn't going to call again right away. Let them wait.

She pulled the folding door open and started toward

the bar, but when she was halfway there she stopped, turned, and went back to the phone booth. As she closed the door she wondered how long the flashers in her car would keep blinking. If they went out, somebody might crash right into her car on the dark road. *So what?* she thought. Serves people right for living out here in the woods where there aren't even any street lights.

"The Walter Hoving Home." It was the sweet young voice again, but this time it didn't fool her. Whoever it was, was tough.

"This is Sandy McKay," she said. It was unmistakably a challenge.

"We've been expecting you, Sandy," the voice said. "Just a minute, please."

Someone else came to the phone. "Hello, Sandy, this is Mrs. Benton. Where are you?"

"On Route 9 somewhere. I think I missed the turnoff to your place. I'm drunk."

"Oh, that's a shame," Mrs. Benton said, as if it really was. "Let's see—can you give me some kind of landmark so I can give you directions from there?"

"My car broke down—right in front of some bar."

"Tell me what your car looks like and we'll come get you."

Crazy. These people were crazy. Sandy wished they would give up and stay home. "I can't leave my car like this," she said.

"We know a very good mechanic. We'll call him before we pick you up."

"Okay," Sandy said. She would see it through. Besides, what else could she do in a town like this, in the middle of the night, with no car? "You'll find me in the bar."

"We'll be there in a few minutes. I don't think you're

far away." Mrs. Benton was just about to say goodbye when Sandy interrupted.

"Wait a minute!" she said. "I was lying before when I said I was drunk. I'm not."

"God bless you, Sandy," Mrs. Benton said, and she seemed to mean that, too. Her sincerity infuriated Sandy.

"But I will be!" she said, slamming the receiver and hoping it knocked off Mrs. Benton's head, too.

CHAPTER 2

Sandy had saved three small pills—one red and two white—for this moment. She had carried them in a pocket of her jeans, and they were cold from the outside air. Sitting at the bar, she held them tightly in her left hand, warming them, as the bartender set a glass of whiskey and ice in front of her.

"Would you mind paying now," he said, his tone making it clear that his words were an order rather than a request. Clearly he didn't like her, and she felt the same way about him. She smiled at him crookedly, enjoying his annoyance, as she pushed a five-dollar bill across the bar. He would have to make change and bring it back to her, which would annoy him even more. That was good. Let him make one wrong remark, and she would throw the drink in his face. The prospect of trouble, especially of her own making, excited her. She felt her heartbeat echoing all through her body, and she was pleased. No one ever suspected that she was so strong, because she was so tiny—barely five feet tall and small-boned, no more than ninety pounds when she was eating well. But when her anger vibrated inside her, when she could feel her blood flowing through her body, she became almost joyfully violent. It was the only way to release the pressure building up inside her.

In the dim orange light of the room she could see her three companions huddled around a pinball machine at the other end of the room. They had forgotten about her. Good. Then they wouldn't miss her when she left. They didn't know what she was doing here, anyway. She laughed to herself, imagining how sometime tomorrow they would suddenly wonder what they were doing in this place and how they would get out of it. Too bad she wouldn't be around to see them.

That reminded her—when she was sure no one was watching her, even in the mirror behind the bar, she lifted her left hand, slid the three pills into her mouth, and washed them down with a swallow of whiskey. When the bartender brought her change she forgot how much she hated him and simply nodded as she stuffed the bills and change into her jacket pocket.

When they came for Sandy she was in a world where no one could reach her. She saw the stocky, red-haired man and the large-eyed blond young woman when they arrived, and she went with them quietly, without even arousing the attention of her three companions at the pinball machine. But part of her was withdrawn, safe behind the stupor the liquor and pills had produced. It was another joke. She was going along with them—and yet she wasn't.

Outside, the red lights from the car's flashers seemed far away, almost pinpoints. Somebody said something about a mechanic—maybe he was already there—but Sandy really didn't care. The red-haired man put his arm through hers and so did the girl, one on each side of her, which helped steady her legs as she allowed them to lead her to a light-colored station wagon pulled up near the doorway.

A dark-haired woman was at the wheel of the wagon, and as Sandy sprawled in the back seat, the woman leaned over and squeezed her hand. "Hi, Sandy," she said. "It's so good to see you!" Something about her manner bothered Sandy, and she pulled her hand away.

"God bless you, dear," the woman said, and then she turned around to start the car.

It was a short ride to wherever they were going, and very dark. Inside and out not a light shone anywhere, except for the dashboard and probing glow from the car's headlights. The glow reached upward as they turned into a steep driveway.

"We're going to heaven," Sandy laughed to herself. "Wait'll they get a look at me there!" But the steepness leveled out, and the car curved around a building and came to a stop.

As they got out, Sandy felt something cold on her face.

"It's starting to snow," the red-haired man said as he took her arm again and led her toward the stairs in front of the building.

In the darkness, broken only by a light at the entrance, Sandy couldn't tell what kind of a building it was, but she guessed it was a house. It had to be a house. What else would you find around there? But it was large, very large. Inside she knew she had never seen such large rooms. Tomorrow, when she felt better, she would pay more attention to what was in them, but right now she just wanted to lie down and be left alone.

She thought they were taking her to a bed, but she was wrong. They let her sit in a big soft chair and then they asked her to empty out her pockets.

"We'll have to go through your pocketbook, too," the man said. "Okay?"

"Those are the rules, Sandy—for everybody," the dark-haired woman explained.

It wasn't okay, Sandy thought—but at least they asked. Nobody else ever had. "Okay, go ahead," she said. They wouldn't find anything. She was much too smart for that.

They put everything on the coffee table in front of her —her cigarettes, a nail clipper, her comb with half the teeth missing, an old lipstick, wads of tissues, some used and some not, a small penknife, some pieces of pretzels, a few bills, and some change.

"Do you have enough money to get back—in case you want to?" said the woman.

"I think so," the man said, counting out the bills. "Unless her car is in big trouble."

"It won't be," Sandy snapped. This was taking much too long. She had to lie down. She couldn't believe it when she saw them tying little white labels on each item on the table. "Look," she said, "I can't wait for you to finish that. Don't I get a room or something?"

"Of course," said the woman. "Oh, you poor baby!" She leaned down and threw her arms around Sandy's thin shoulders. This time Sandy did not pull back, although she had to force herself to sit still.

"Snow's already beginning to stick," she heard someone say as a hand grasped hers and helped her out of her chair. Quickly now she was losing all awareness of her surroundings as her mind sought a familiar numbness. She felt herself being led away from the large room into a darker part of the building, with walls close to her—perhaps a hallway—and then there was a door, and beyond it a bed. She dropped onto it before the bedspread could be removed. Someone was putting a blanket over her, tucking it close to her body. She wanted to tell whoever it was not to bother—she wasn't cold—but by that time she was too far away to be heard.

The first sound Sandy heard when she awoke was no sound at all. Accustomed to city noises, the silence of the country night was frightening. Sandy ran her nails along the nubby surface of the bedspread, and the sound of her scratching seemed incredibly loud. But she *was* awake. She was not dreaming that she had fallen into some kind of noiseless, motionless atmosphere. She was in a dark room, its furniture silhouetted by a strange pale light that even the window shade could not keep out.

She was cold now, so she pulled the blanket around her as she sat up and went to the window. Pulling aside the shade at one side, she looked out cautiously, careful not to show her face at the window. The light came from the whiteness that covered everything she could see—the ground, the trees, and beyond the trees to what must have been a mountain. Then she remembered the snow. She lifted the shade, no longer afraid to expose herself at the window, and pressed her face to the glass, shielding her eyes from the reflection. Yes, it was still snowing, and that made her uneasy.

She felt very weak and went back to the bed where she sat down, pulling the blanket tighter around her. It didn't help. She was beginning to shiver. Now she was sorry she had ever come here. She wasn't ready to go through with it.

She pulled up her legs and lay down on the bed, but she felt nauseous and sat up again quickly, wondering where the bathroom was.

She saw a sliver of light under a door and headed for it,

but she stumbled over a chair. Swearing, she leaned down to rub her throbbing shin and felt very dizzy. As she straightened up, the door opened and two girls came in.

"It's okay, Sandy, let's get you back in bed," one of them said as she took Sandy's arm and turned her around.

"I'm sick!" Sandy said, pulling her arm free.

"We know," the girl said. "We know how you feel."

They helped her into the hallway, moving quietly on each side of her. A few minutes later, in the immaculate, white-tiled bathroom, she began to vomit and knew she would not stop for a long time. But these crazy people stayed there with her, wiping her face again and again with a cold, wet cloth. At first she thought they were talking to each other, probably about her, until she realized that they actually were praying. She couldn't believe it. Now she *knew* they were not right in the head—prayers were for the proper places in life, for churches and people who got all dressed up on Sunday.

As the girls helped Sandy back to her room and brought more blankets to still her shuddering, she decided she had been wrong to come here. She had to get away, go back to where she had been, bad as that was. They *didn't* understand how it was with her. She felt as if she were going to die.

"Where's a telephone?" she said, pushing away the blankets and forcing herself to sit up. She was so cold that her teeth chattered as she spoke, but that didn't matter. She had to get out.

"In the reception room," one of the girls said softly. "To your right, at the end of the hall."

No one tried to stop her as she left the bedroom and walked down the long hallway to the large room that she remembered from a few hours earlier. The girls followed close behind her—*and they were still praying!* It was a crazy house.

There was a telephone on the wall across the room, and as Sandy went toward it she began to feel stronger with each step she took. But why the telephone? She couldn't remember why she wanted it. Her mind was still fuzzy.

The mechanic—yes, that was why. She couldn't go anywhere unless she had her car.

"What's the mechanic's number?" she said and found only one girl standing behind her. There were tears in the girl's eyes.

"We'll get it for you—Lois just went to get Mrs. Benton, and she'll tell you. But Sandy—we wish you'd stay—try it for a day, at least."

Sandy pushed the girl away roughly. She knew that if she didn't get out of there fast she would begin to break something. And Mrs. Benton might get hurt if she tried to mother her again.

Mrs. Benton seemed to know better—at least *she* wasn't crazy. She simply asked Sandy if she was sure she wanted to leave, and then she called the mechanic.

"He won't have your car until late in the afternoon," Mrs. Benton said, and when Sandy glared at her, she explained, "I got him up out of bed—it's four o'clock in the morning, Sandy. He hasn't done any work on the car yet."

Sandy could do better, she knew she could. These people were too soft. But when she asked for the mechanic's phone number they refused to give it to her.

"Wait until a decent hour and then you can have it," Mrs. Benton said. "That's fair, Sandy."

Fair. She was dying and they were talking about being fair. She looked around the room desperately, wondering if she could get into town on foot.

Mrs. Benton read her thoughts. "It's still snowing," she said.

"Tell you what, Sandy," Mrs. Benton said, "we'll make a

deal—okay? Wait here until eight o'clock, and I'll drive you to the garage for your car. You can stay there until it's fixed. How's that?"

Sandy shrugged and dug her hands hard into the pockets of her jeans. She had no choice and she knew it, but she wondered how she would live through four more hours with these freaks. Things would get worse, not better, because she could feel the cramps beginning in her stomach.

"Okay," she said. She had to sit down before the cramps bent her in two.

"Oh, Sandy, we love you!" Mrs. Benton said, but she kept her distance. So did the two girls. They sat on a couch opposite her and began to pray again, just the way they used to do it when she knew them years ago, in Brooklyn.

Sandy was in her early twenties then, and older than most of the other young people who used to heckle the Bentons when they held their street meetings. They came from an organization called Teen Challenge, which Sandy knew very well from some of her friends. At least they *were* her friends until they started listening to those Bible verses the Teen Challenge people were always quoting.

One by one her friends went over to the other side, and before very long they were out on the street with the Bentons trying to preach to *her*. Some of the toughest ones gave in—even Nicky Cruz, who used to run the biggest gang in Brooklyn. That really surprised Sandy. She could remember the days of the gang fights when her own brother used to fight at Nicky Cruz's side. Sandy was a little girl then, but by the time she grew up there weren't any gangs. Some people said it was drugs that broke them up because once a person was high he didn't want to fight. Maybe so, but Sandy couldn't help thinking that people like the Bentons and groups like Teen Challenge had also helped to destroy the gangs. They were jealous of the gangs because they gave the neighborhood young people something they needed. In those days a girl could walk down the street without worrying who was going to jump out of an alley and stick a knife in her back—if anything happened to her, she had friends who would settle the score. The do-gooders didn't understand such things. They thought the world was a nice place to be, where everyone obeyed the rules and crossed when the light was green. They didn't know what it was to be afraid of dark hallways even in the daytime, of running footsteps and sudden cries on the roof at night. The do-gooders lived in pretty little houses where they left the doors unlocked at night and the keys in the car.

So when Sandy lost a friend to the preachers it meant that she lost part of her security, and she had very little left. She hated the sight of the Bentons, and whenever she found them talking to a girl or a boy on the streets she screamed at them in the foulest words she knew. They never got angry. They were embarrassed—who wouldn't be?—but that didn't seem to bother them. They even tried to be nice to her. Sandy was so frustrated by their lack of hostility that one time when she found them taking a coffee break in a luncheonette she walked over to them and spat at them. Big tears fell from Mrs. Benton's eyes as she said, "Oh, Sandy, you need God's love so badly—won't you let him give it to you?"

Sandy turned and ran away. After that she kept her distance when the Bentons were on the street, although she didn't know why she was afraid of them.

Afraid? No, it wasn't fear. She wasn't afraid of anything, and to prove it to herself one day she walked right into the Teen Challenge headquarters just to look it over. She expected to be thrown out and was ready to make it a memorable occasion, but nothing like that happened. Inside the old brick house on Clinton Avenue, where Teen Challenge founder David Wilkerson was supposed to have his office, she saw many familiar faces. Some of them used to be her friends, but when they came toward her, smiling and holding out their arms, she told them to leave her alone. She saw John Benton there—you couldn't miss his red hair. He was talking to a thin blond man in jeans and a pullover sweater, and when he saw Sandy, he waved to her.

"Hey, Sandy, I want you to meet somebody," he said, and the blond man looked in her direction. She recognized him immediately. It was Wilkerson. She had seen him enough times when he walked the streets of her neighborhood with Nicky Cruz at his side. The sight of them together had made her brother sick. In a way, Sandy blamed them for her brother's death in a fight after Nicky left the gang. If Nicky had been there it wouldn't have happened—he used to take care of her brother.

"John tells me you used to know Nicky Cruz," the blond man said to her. Sandy resented his friendliness. She didn't like the way his blue eyes never left her face, as if he were searching for something. Whatever it was, Sandy didn't want him to find it.

"Sure," she said, giving him her lopsided smile. "I knew him when he was a man—that was before you turned him into a crybaby."

David Wilkerson was just like the rest of them—he smiled at her. "I didn't do anything to Nicky," he said, "but God turned him into a pretty wonderful person."

"He's a louse," Sandy said, and inside herself she was admiring the calm way she stood there, getting back at this Wilkerson.

"He's a minister now—did you know that?"

"Who cares?"

"I think *you* do, Sandy. I think you care a lot about what happened to Nicky, because maybe you'd like the same thing to happen to you." He was *worse* than the Bentons! What made him think he knew what went on inside her?

"You're sick! Do you know that?" She was screaming now, and she felt her pulse getting stronger. Soon, very soon, she would explode and find that wonderful relief.

"Sandy, you need help," John Benton said. "You can't be having such a good time with all that hate inside you."

"I don't need anything—except for you to leave me alone! Stay out of my streets and keep away from my friends!" For some reason she wanted to get away before she began smashing things. It wasn't that she cared what happened to them—she just had to get away. And so she ran.

Every now and then she went back to the house on Clinton Avenue, always with the intention of starting trouble, but never succeeding. Finally she gave up the battle and turned her attention to other things. She had to go one way or the other, and she certainly wasn't going to go over to the Bentons. Instead she went the way some of her other friends had gone, except that instead of taking heroin and hashish and pot, she took pills. She began taking them because she didn't sleep well, but that was only an excuse, and she knew it. She took them to stop living and yet to keep from dying. But every now and then, especially when things went wrong, she thought of the Bentons and wondered if they were still praying for her. If they were, their prayers sure weren't working, because hardly anything ever went right for Sandy. Her father still came home drunk every night and beat up her mother. Somehow he managed to hold onto his job, but his drinking kept the family in poverty. Sandy's older sister took an overdose of heroin and came out of it with no mind at all. And Sandy herself—well, she was so busy trying to stay asleep that she made some bad mistakes. One of them was getting pregnant. At least she thought it was a mistake at the time, but when she gave birth to a dark-haired little girl, she changed her mind. Holding the warm-blanketed infant in her arms, Sandy felt proud of what her body had nourished. Of course, she had to give her up. Joe, the child's father, was hiding from the police, and even Sandy didn't know where he was. One day he would show up, as he always did, but he wouldn't want anything to do with a child. In fact, Sandy didn't want him to know about his daughter. The child had to have a better chance in life.

Sandy named the girl Hope and consented to put her in a foster home, but only after a social worker assured her that she would be placed with a family who really wanted a child and would bring her up as if she were their own. Although she couldn't go so far as to give up her daughter for adoption, Sandy didn't try to play games with herself. She knew she would never be a fit mother, and this little girl was a special human being. But she wanted to be able to keep an eye on her child, and perhaps, when she was in good shape, keep in touch with her.

As soon as it was light, Sandy was at the window. The snow had stopped falling, but it was several inches deep on the ground. The two girls were still with her, but Mrs. Benton was gone.

The whole house came to life a few minutes later as girls came into the reception room from every direction. Some, who obviously lived in the house itself, wore heavy sweaters and jeans, and others, who must have come from another building, wore heavy coats and stomped the snow off their boots before they came inside. Most of them were laughing and joking with each other. Almost every one of them smiled at Sandy as they passed through the reception room into the dining room, which Sandy could see from where she stood. She refused to smile back.

"What time is it?" she asked one of the girls who had sat up with her.

"Seven-thirty. Would you like something to eat?"

"No. Where's Mrs. Benton?"

"She'll be here. It isn't eight o'clock yet, Sandy."

Sandy laughed. "You're something. You really are something. I don't suppose you'd consider getting me out of here a few minutes early?"

"You'll be lucky to get out at all in this snow."

"I'll get out, don't worry."

She couldn't stand the sounds from the dining room, and she turned her back on the sight of the girls crowded around small tables, talking excitedly and occasionally breaking into happy laughter. But she couldn't get away from the noise when they stood up clapping rhythmically, and shouted a girl's name, demanding that she come in from the kitchen. Sandy turned around and saw a tall, thin girl with glasses looking most reluctantly into the dining room. Suddenly she was greeted by cheers and applause. The girl's hands went to her cheeks, and she smiled delightedly.

Sandy turned to the girl sitting on the couch.

"This is MaryAnn's first week on kitchen duty, and she didn't think she could do the work," the girl explained before Sandy could ask the question. "The girls are trying to tell her she was wrong—she did just fine."

"What is this, a kindergarten?" Sandy sneered. "They act like a bunch of babies!"

"They are—in a way," the girl said, smiling. She was going to say more but changed her mind.

At exactly eight by the clock over the large stone mantel in the room, Mrs. Benton came downstairs dressed in a warm coat, heavy wool pants, and a knitted hat, which she pulled down over her ears. She handed Sandy a bulky green sweater.

"You're not wearing much for this kind of weather," Mrs. Benton said. "Put this on under your jacket—maybe it'll help."

When Sandy shook her head proudly, Mrs. Benton said, "It's not charity, and it doesn't belong to anybody. Lots of people send us their used clothing, and we just help ourselves whenever we need something. I think it will fit you. It's the smallest one I could find."

Sandy's mind was beginning to function more clearly now, and she realized she might have to spend hours out in the cold before her car was repaired. She couldn't afford to say no, but she accepted the gift with contempt, holding it gingerly as she examined it for holes and signs of wear. It looked brand new. She put it on, grimacing as if in pain and refusing to acknowledge its warm comfort. Then she put her jacket on over it.

"Okay, let's go," she said to Mrs. Benton.

"Just a minute," Mrs. Benton said and hurried into the kitchen. She came back immediately with a cardboard box that had once housed a cake. "In case you get hungry," she said, offering the box to Sandy and smiling as if the occasion were a happy one. "It's only a sandwich and some fruit." She had the most unusual and beautiful eyes Sandy had ever seen—light green and turned up at the corners, always ready to smile. Her attitude was so contagious that Sandy smiled back at her as she took the box, and then she caught herself up sharply. If they wanted to keep her from starving to death, she wasn't going to argue with them.

"Come on," Sandy said, turning toward the front door. "Let me out of this place!"

CHAPTER 3

"This place" was The Walter Hoving Home in Garrison, New York, a little more than an hour's drive from Manhattan. It is a shelter, a training ground, a rehabilitation center for young women with some of the most serious problems in the world. Drug addicts, prostitutes, criminals, runaways, and delinquents have been coming here since the Home was opened in the summer of 1967. Most of them come because, like Sandy, they don't have anywhere else to go. They have run out of chances and think they might as well give this one a try. They come, not eagerly and filled with hope for a recovery, but desperately, angrily, challenging the staff to give them a reason and a way to go on living. Many, like Sandy, don't stay. But some do, and 90 per cent of those who remain go on to build new and worthwhile lives.

Ninety per cent is a very high rate of cure, much higher than any other rehabilitation program can claim. And in the Home itself there are other differences.

"I've been to them all," said a girl who came in recently, "Daytop, Synanon, state hospitals, federal programs. They treated me like dirt. Here, they give me love. The religious part doesn't bother me—because they really mean it."

The "religious part" is the major portion of the Home's program. "Jesus Christ is the one who works the miracles," says Rev. John Benton, the Home's director, "not us. We just try to do what we feel he wants us to do."

For John Benton the Home began long before he ever heard of Garrison, New York. It began as a pain in his spirit every time he saw a girl in trouble. Girls have it so much rougher than boys, he realized. There are so many more ways they can go wrong. Take addicts, for example. A boy might have to steal something to get money for drugs, but a girl just had to walk down a city street until she found a man looking for a good time.

Early in their marriage, John and his wife, Elsie, had opened their home to troubled girls, but they could take in only one at a time. They knew what God's love could do to rebuild a ravaged life, and it was their dream to find a way to offer that love on a larger scale.

One day, quite unexpectedly, the dream began to come true. John and Elsie had moved from Seattle to Long Island, New York, when John became crusade director for Teen Challenge, the ministry to young people founded by David Wilkerson. John was excited about working with Dave, but organizing crusades just didn't seem to be his talent. At least he didn't think so. He tried a few other things, such as editing the monthly newsletter and counseling, but he didn't feel he was particularly effective at either one. "I'm especially bad at counseling," he told Dave. "When I talk to some of these young boys and girls for an hour, I'm a wreck. The pain they've gone through—it gets to me, and I can't keep from crying. I don't know how I can help anybody that way."

Dave Wilkerson also was worried about the girls who came to Teen Challenge. They needed a program especially designed for their problems. They needed personal, individual attention from compassionate Christians who could make an institution feel like a home. That spelled the Bentons. Would John and Elsie be willing to give up their home in Long Island and move to Brooklyn, to a red-brick house across the street from Teen Challenge headquarters on Clinton Avenue? For them, it would mean giving up a lot. They had three young children of their own, and Clinton Avenue was in a dangerous neighborhood. The Bentons would have to share their home with as many delinquent girls as they could fit into its rooms.

The answer, from all the Bentons was an immediate, enthusiastic Yes!

During the next two years that enthusiasm was eaten away by frustration. Money was always a problem, and so was space. Only nine girls could be accommodated at the home—which as yet had no name. Nine was a lot more than one, Elsie Benton kept reminding herself, but as she walked the streets at night with her husband and other Teen Challenge workers, she realized that nine was not enough.

Of course, there was a big turnover. Most of the girls couldn't take the discipline that was a vital part of the program. Some of them couldn't face going through withdrawal from drugs without the aid of medication. Some couldn't adjust to regular hours and three meals a day. Rebellious girls who had had trouble with their own families found it difficult to fit into the family atmosphere of the Home. There were scenes, arguments, angry departures, and each time it hurt the Bentons just as much as the first time. Always there was the hope that a dropout would return—which she could do as often as she wanted. Sometimes it happened, and sometimes the girl stayed. But there were those other times when the Bentons learned that a girl who had dropped out ended up in jail—or dead. *Could we have done more?* the Bentons asked themselves. They never were sure.

Perhaps they weren't doing as much as they had hoped, or as quickly as they had dreamed, but they knew they were going in the right direction. They had seen girls change from miserable, hostile, depressed creatures to strong, determined, charming young women. As the months went by, more girls were completing the program, and the program itself began to change. The Bentons weren't as easily fooled by the theatrical abilities of the girls. They knew that some of the girls would try to smuggle drugs into the Home as security in case they found withdrawal too painful, so they searched a girl's belongings before they admitted her. They did it openly, with the girl's permission and in her presence. They made the rules more restrictive—a girl couldn't leave the Home for any reason whatsoever unless she was in the company of a staff member. The city made it too easy for a girl to get her hands on money—the subway was just down the street, and often that was as far as a girl had to go. Drug pushers were everywhere, even in the apartment building next door to the Home. Stealing, which was a way of life for many of the girls, was a special problem. They stole from the staff and from each other, and the only way the Bentons found to deal with it was honest confrontation. If the girl confessed, she was forgiven and allowed to return the stolen article. But if the girl lied and denied a theft, she was told to leave—not angrily, but with earnest prayers for her to face the truth and return.

The Home, like the rest of the Teen Challenge program, was supported by donations, some large and many small. There never was enough money for all the things that had to be done, and so John Benton was surprised when Dave Wilkerson told him to look around for a new location for the girls' home. They needed a place in the country, Wilkerson told him, somewhere far away from the temptations of the city, a quiet place where they could hear the voice of God more clearly. John Benton agreed. In fact, Wilkerson was describing Benton's constant prayer, one he had been reluctant to voice because he didn't know where they would get the money for such a home. What Dave Wilkerson meant was a country estate, a mansion.

Actually, the idea wasn't as farfetched as it seemed. Country estates were so expensive to maintain that many of them were selling for prices far below their worth. Somebody's white elephant might come to the rescue.

But, again, the money . . .

Wilkerson didn't seem to be worried about that. God would find a way.

John Benton had seen Dave Wilkerson like this before. When Wilkerson felt certain that God wanted him to do something, he simply began doing it, confident that God would remove any obstacles. And God always did. But John Benton wasn't as sure that he knew what God wanted him to do. He couldn't always tell whether his ideas were his own or God's—some of them, as it turned out, were much too foolish to be anything but his. And so he went forward in a different manner, a little more cautiously, one foot in front of the other, and was never particularly surprised when he was turned back. He regarded an insurmountable obstacle as a signal to try another way. To some, he may have seemed lacking in confidence, but he made up for it in persistence. He never seemed to run out of "another way," and eventually he got to where God apparently wanted him to be, although he never quite knew how he got there. He was absolutely sincere in his claim that "the Lord did it, not I."

For months Elsie and John Benton read the real-estate columns in the newspapers and followed up anything that was promising within reach of New York. The one thing that was missing in most of the properties they went to see was enough bedrooms. An ordinary estate—if there was such a thing—would not do. They needed something special. Finally they thought they had found it in a town called Garrison, just north of Bear Mountain and West Point in New York State.

The nearest city of any size was Peekskill, fifteen miles to the south. The house itself was large enough. It had been a health resort and was surrounded by acres of beautiful lawns and trees. There was a swimming pool and even a sauna bath. And plenty of rooms!

The only problem was the price. The owners were asking $100,000, and John Benton had a budget of $60,000.

When the Bentons showed the property to Wilkerson, he didn't think much of it. He found something wrong with the roof, something that would have meant expensive repairs, and he pointed out that the frame construction would also be difficult to maintain. He had seen another property across the road that was much more appealing. "That's the place you ought to have," he said, as if it were only a matter of selection.

"The place you ought to have" was a three-story stone house on almost twenty-three acres of the most beautiful land John Benton had ever seen. A stream lined with stones meandered through the hills, and at one point it had been diverted into a natural swimming pool. The property was for sale, for $225,000.

The house had been used most recently as a convalescent home for members of the union that owned it. It had fifteen bedrooms and nine bathrooms and came complete with furniture, linens, kitchen utensils—everything. But the price, of course, was unthinkable.

Nevertheless, the two ministers made an appointment to look at the property. Wilkerson thought they might get the price down a little, but Benton wondered how that would help; it was so far from the $60,000 he could spend. But, one foot in front of the other, he followed his friend, who seemed to be much more certain where they were going.

In a rose garden at the bottom of the hill on which the house was built, the two men stopped. The setting was so lovely that they simply had to pause. It was so different from the environment the girls shared in the city—nature itself could minister to them here.

Wilkerson looked at Benton. *This was the new home for the girls,* he said. This was where God wanted them to be. Benton's mouth felt dry. If only *he* could be that sure!

Wilkerson wanted to pray. "Let's believe that God is going to give this place for the girls," he said, as he bowed his head. In his prayer he told God he was claiming the property for him. He did not doubt in the slightest that God would do something about the price of it.

And God did.

The union brought the price down to $175,000, which still seemed astronomical to John Benton. But then the union agreed to accept a $20,000 down payment from Teen Challenge and carry the mortgage themselves. Annual mortgage payments would come to about $10,000, plus interest, and the first year's payment didn't have to be made until December 31—almost a year away!

On June 23, 1967, the Bentons and four other members

of the staff moved into the big house in Garrison. With them they brought twelve girls, already three more than they could have accommodated in Brooklyn. It was a beautiful day. The sun was warm, and a soft breeze rustled the leaves on the trees, promising a cool evening. They were like children, the staff and the girls, moving excitedly from one room to another, amazed that there always seemed to be still more unexplored corners of the house. They ran down some of the hills and climbed back up, falling breathlessly on the grass. For some of the girls, it was the first time they had ever been able to pick flowers, and at dinner that evening there were bright bouquets on each table in the dining room.

The dining room, Elsie Benton decided, would soon be too small. But that could be changed in time. The Bentons' own quarters—a single room that served as bedroom and sitting room—would also be cramped. That, too, could be remedied later. Now it was more important to fill those empty bedrooms.

The last thing that passed through John Benton's mind that night before he fell into a deep sleep was the happy knowledge that they all were where God wanted them to be. Even in his sleep he seemed to be offering thanks.

CHAPTER 4

Some men could account for the exact moment when they decided to enter the ministry. The "call" from God had been clear and unmistakable. It was not so with John Benton. He knew that if God had called him, he had not been listening, and God therefore had to resort to other methods.

John's parents were devout Christians. His father, once an alcoholic, credited Jesus Christ with curing him. John's older brothers accepted their parents' faith—but not John. During his middle teens John went through a period of skepticism. He thought he could take pretty good care of himself.

The United States was caught up in the Korean conflict when John approached draft age. Although his brothers had gone into service without a murmur, John objected. He never said it in so many words, but he simply didn't want to risk getting killed. Since he was unmarried, with no prospects of a serious romance, that form of deferment was out. But if he decided to become a minister—ah, that was the answer! When he finished high school he would enroll in a seminary. In the meantime he got a job with an evangelist who preached in the Seattle area.

One day John met a pretty young girl who attended

one of the revival meetings. Her name was Elsie, and there was something special about her. They began to see each other as much as they could in the short intervals between John's trips up and down the West Coast. John noticed that when he was away from Elsie something was gone out of his life. Although he hadn't known her long, he had better not risk losing her. He made up his mind when he was on a trip to Alaska, so he called Elsie and asked her to marry him. She said yes, and neither of them could see any reason for a long engagement. They were married a few weeks after John came back from Alaska.

But what about seminary? And the draft? John had forgotten about his earlier plans. Now they seemed obsolete, poorly suited for a married man. Elsie disagreed. She wanted him to go to seminary and was willing to get a job. She didn't expect to make much money, but it would be enough. Somehow she had the feeling that seminary was where her husband ought to be.

She was right. In seminary, John Benton was forced to reckon with the Bible. He had read it before, but never studiously. Now, as he began to struggle with its deeper meaning, going from one translation to the next and following the thoughts of scholars in the commentaries, he was caught more than called by God. This was no ordinary book. This was the Word of God himself. Its message was as relevant to life today as it was in the beginning of time. "God so loved the world that he gave his only begotten son. . . ."

By the time John graduated he was, in every fiber of his being, a minister, dedicated to telling everyone he could reach about the love of God for man. This love was something he could describe realistically, because he himself had been changed by it. For one thing, he wasn't afraid to die, because he knew that death was the beginning, not the end, of life. Jesus Christ had already died for him—and for every other man and woman who would accept Jesus' sacrifice—and offered him, instead, eternity. No, John didn't want to leave Elsie and the child they were about to have, but he knew he could trust God to make that decision. As for him, he went to the draft board and asked them to reactivate his draft status. There was still fighting in Korea, and John wanted to join his brothers.

The draft board refused. John was a minister and he was about to become a father, two reasons for deferment. Rules were rules. God was turning him back.

John had the feeling that he wasn't ready for a congregation. Perhaps he never would be. He couldn't see himself as an administrator. He wanted to move around, to find people who didn't know that God loved them. The trouble was, they were everywhere, even in church. Where could he serve best?

For a while John worked with Campus Crusade for Christ. He liked working with young people, and he knew that just because a boy or a girl was well dressed, had a car and enough money to spend, it didn't mean that everything was right with the world. A cashmere sweater couldn't nourish a hungry spirit.

John knew about David Wilkerson's work, and he was eager to meet him when he heard that Dave was coming to address a Campus Crusade rally. But he was totally unprepared for the offer Dave made him the day after the rally. "Come and work with us at Teen Challenge, John," Wilkerson said. "You have no idea how much I need a good assistant—I've been asking God to lead me to the right man. He just did."

Wilkerson was so direct, so confident of God's will, that John knew he would have to accept. Elsie agreed.

But Wilkerson didn't get an assistant for long, and John Benton, who never considered himself an administrator, found himself struggling to keep a home for girls from going bankrupt.

Although the Home was affiliated with Teen Challenge, it was on its own when it came to finances. That was only fair. Teen Challenge had a lot of other responsibilities. If the Home had a reason to be, it would survive. John accepted that fact of life until a few weeks before the end of the year, when he realized that the first annual mortgage payment was soon due.

They didn't have ten thousand dollars. The contributions that had trickled in were consumed by the upkeep costs and the increased number of girls they accepted. Was it possible that the Home would go broke in its first year?

As John Benton searched his mind for another way, he remembered another money crisis earlier that year, before the move to Garrison. The Home simply didn't have enough money to keep operating.

"Talk to Walter Hoving," Wilkerson had said.

Walter Hoving, chairman of the board of Tiffany & Co. in New York City, had been an early supporter of Teen Challenge. He and his wife, Pauline, had given more than their money, their time, and their love. They were determined to achieve nothing less than the goals the organization had set for itself—and their toughness was contagious.

"Let me think about it," Hoving had said when John Benton told him how desperately the Home needed money. In a few days he called Benton and gave him the name of a foundation, a man to call, and a telephone number. "Don't go telling anyone which foundation it is.

They don't want to be swamped with requests they can't fill. But call. Now."

Benton called. An appointment was arranged. And after the representative of the foundation learned what was happening at the girls' home, he approved a donation of fifteen thousand dollars.

Would he do it again? John Benton wondered. Well, now was the time to find out. He made a call and arranged to see the representative.

Benton was concerned only with the immediate need: the first annual mortgage payment. The foundation representative had something more in mind. There would be other annual payments for many years to come. Suppose the foundation were to guarantee enough money to meet the mortgage payments each year until the property was paid off?

Benton was astonished.

There was only one problem: the foundation had already given a donation to the Home that year. It was not their policy to give twice to any group in a calendar year.

Benton felt as if he had been hit in the stomach. How much better it would have been just to be turned back in the beginning.

But, the foundation representative went on, there was a way to work things out. The mortgage payment was due on December 31, the last day of the year, which happened to be a Sunday. The next day, January 1, was a holiday. If the foundation sent Benton a check on January 2, would that be all right?

Benton smiled. Every Christmas carol he had ever heard began to ring in his ears. Unashamed of his joy, he grasped the man's hand and said, "Praise the Lord!"

Driving back to Garrison that evening, he had to agree

with his former opinion of himself. He was *not* a good administrator. But that didn't seem to make much difference.

The Home was self-supporting, at least as far as the roof over its head was concerned. Now it ought to have a name of its own. Benton called the foundation representative and asked him if he had any suggestions.

"Why not call it the Hoving Home?" was the reply, in honor of Walter Hoving's seventieth birthday. After all, it was Hoving who had spoken to the widow of the man who had set up the foundation. It was he who had persuaded her that the Home was worthy of the help she could give it.

Benton liked the idea. In fact, it had occurred to him earlier that year, and Mrs. Hoving agreed that it was appropriate. But Walter Hoving would have no part of it. "Nonsense," he said, waving the suggestion away with a sweep of his hand. "I haven't done anything worth memorializing. You know as well as I do that Jesus Christ got you that home, and he's the one who'll keep it going."

But now Hoving couldn't possibly refuse, Benton realized. It was the foundation's request that he lend his name to the Home. "This time you can't say no," Benton said when he called Walter Hoving.

"Well, I guess not."

"Good! Then it's official—we'll call it The Walter Hoving Home."

CHAPTER 5

Bill Roach owned some property across the road from The Walter Hoving Home. He spent a lot of time there, keeping up the grounds and the buildings, but he lived in a small white-frame house in the neighboring town of Cold Spring. He was not exactly happy when he heard about the purpose of the Home. A lot of delinquent girls coming to Garrison? That might mean trouble.

Garrison is a community of thirty-six hundred residents. Their houses are quite far apart, and the atmosphere could be called rural except for the absence of farms and the presence of old estates. In the early part of the century, when there was money to be made in railroads, it was fashionable for railroad executives to build elaborate stone homes in the old mountain ranges within reach of the city. They were cool retreats for wives and children in the summer, and the men came up each Friday night to spend the weekend. Eventually the railroad connections were good enough for men to live in the mountains all year round. The skiing, tobogganing, and sleigh riding were wonderful, and the sight of the unspoiled, glistening snow was uplifting, in contrast to the increasing grime of city life.

The estate houses were huge. Labor was cheap—a dollar a day in many places—and men were eager for work. Immigrants from all over the world, many with extraordinary skills and talents, were coming to America in unprecedented numbers, and there was hardly anything that they could not do. One had only to dream and, with a little money, the dream became a reality. Consequently the houses boasted some of the finest wood carvings, stained glass, cut stone, and mortaring ever seen. Sometimes the architecture was a little outlandish because an owner dreamed a bit too extravagantly, but never mind. Even if a turret suddenly erupted from the straight line of a roof, or a too-sharp angle of a gable forced a room into a strange shape, or an excessive amount of wood paneling made a room dim in the daylight, the craftmanship itself was always beautiful.

Once the homes had been maintainable. When wages were low, domestic help was easy to obtain, even in the country, and the huge estates were kept in immaculate condition by staffs of many servants. The acres and acres of land surrounding each house were turned into lovely gardens separated by curving pathways and clusters of trees. Lawns always looked freshly mowed, and shrubs were cut into geometrical shapes, with never a leaf out of place.

But that was another day. Now the estates were burdens for most of the families who inherited them. The cost of domestic help was too high, and the glorious acreage, once a feast for the eye, had become a tax problem. One by one the properties were being sold.

Most of the new buyers were not individuals or families. They were institutions, many of them religious. They were attracted by the low selling price and had the manpower to keep up the property. Good for them—but not so good for their neighbors.

As Bill Roach put it, it didn't seem fair for these institutions to be buying up so much Garrison property. The institutions didn't have to pay taxes—most of them were nonprofit organizations—which meant that the rest of the property owners in the community had to make up the difference. And as Roach pointed out, suppose the institutions decided to sell the property a few years later? They could walk off with the profits.

Roach had nothing against The Walter Hoving Home itself. But he was concerned about the practical issues.

Some of the other neighbors reacted more emotionally. When two young girls were seen walking along a road, the word spread that drug addicts were straying off their property. Although it turned out that the girls didn't even live at The Walter Hoving Home, but rather at an orphanage nearby, the damage had already been done. John Benton didn't actually see it happen, but he was told by some of the girls that one of the neighbors was patrolling the border of his property with a gun and threatened to use it if one of the girls stepped over onto his land.

Benton was uneasy. He knew what it was to be ignorant of the facts about addiction. Before he joined Dave Wilkerson in Brooklyn, Benton had never seen a drug addict. *And what we don't understand, we fear,* he thought. His neighbors were afraid, and they might make rash decisions. Being able to pay the mortgage on the big stone house did not mean that the girls could stay there. They still had to be approved—even accepted—by the community. There still was a Certificate of Occupancy that had to be issued by the town. Ordinarily that would be a formality, but if the occupants of the house were not welcome, the certificate might be denied. In other words, the girls had to do more than the average person moving into

Garrison. They had to prove themselves good citizens—or get out.

Benton wanted to meet the problem head-on. The trouble was, he didn't know quite where to begin.

Not all the neighbors were opposed to the Home. A short distance away and up a road that wound for almost two miles around a mountain, there was a house everybody called "the castle." It was a large stone building with a magnificent view of the Hudson River, and it was called a castle because, with its wings and towers, it truly looked like one. The house was built in 1880 by William Church Osborn, whose great-grandson, Alexander Perry Osborn, Jr., lived there now.

Perry Osborn and his wife, Marian, also had heard the rumors. They had visited the Home when it opened. They knew the Bentons, the staff, and many of the girls. They were impressed with the work that was being done there, and they hoped it could continue.

The Osborns were no strangers to addiction or to most other forms of affliction. Perry Osborn was a director of the Burke Rehabilitation Center in White Plains, New York, where he spent many of his working hours trying to solve the problems involved in the care of patients with long-term illnesses. He knew how hard it was for a handicapped person to make any progress at all and how much time it took for improvement to become visible. He knew, too, what a strain the effort was on both patient and therapist—the anxious trying, the almost superhuman effort, finally the inching forward, and often the long fall backward. The girls who came to the Home were like the patients at Burke—except that their sickness usually was in their soul and more difficult to treat.

Marian Osborn, a slim, intense, handsome woman, was

impatient. "Somebody had better do something about these rumors," she said to her husband one evening as they were discussing the latest story about "the wild girls from the Home."

Then she leaned forward in her chair. "Why don't *we*?"

"Do something?" her husband said. "Got any ideas?"

"Yes!" she said excitedly. "I think we ought to have a meeting—of all our neighbors—here. Let's invite the Bentons and some of the girls from the Home, and let everybody see that we're dealing with real people, not monsters."

"Fine!" Perry said as he stood up. "I'll call John and Elsie about it—you start calling the neighbors."

CHAPTER 6

Marian Osborn knew it would not be difficult to get people to come to the meeting. Everybody was curious about the castle, and those who had been there usually wanted to come again. But there was a limit to the number of people who could be accommodated in one room, and it was important for everyone to hear what was said. The living room, with its huge fireplace, oak-paneled walls, and large windows was both spacious and warm, two important elements. After the meeting, refreshments could be served in the sitting room across the hall.

Obviously not every resident of Garrison could be invited, so Marian decided to ask only those who lived in the vicinity of the Home. They were the ones who were panicking. She also invited some of the community officials.

"Ask the Hovings if they'd like to come, too," Perry suggested.

"Good idea," Marian said, looking up the number in her address book. The Osborns and the Hovings had known each other for years.

On a Sunday afternoon a few days later the castle entrance was crowded with early arrivals. Mildred Losee, the Osborns' housekeeper, had had most of the furniture removed from the living room and replaced with folding chairs arranged in rows facing the fireplace. It was a sunny fall day, and the light coming through the tall, paned windows was cheerful.

About sixty people had taken seats when the Bentons arrived. With them was Walter Hoving, a tanned, slender man, well over six feet tall, and two young girls. As they took their seats near the front of the room, the girls glanced around nervously. Elsie Benton reached across her husband to squeeze their hands reassuringly. Walter Hoving got up several times to shake hands with acquaintances. To each he said a few words, bending close to the other person's ear to be heard above the conversations around them.

Perry Osborn walked to the front of the room and held up his hands for silence. He described the purpose of the meeting and introduced the group from the Home to their neighbors. "That's really why we're here," he said, "to get to know each other." Then he opened the meeting to questions.

There were a few. They came slowly, awkwardly. Most of them were practical considerations, such as the ones Bill Roach had raised.

"I agree with your concern," John Benton answered. "We don't want to use your community—we want to be *part* of it. So we've made a special arrangement: If at any future time we should sell this property and make a profit, we will pay our share of taxes for the time we have lived here."

"Fair enough," someone said, and several voices grunted agreement.

Gradually the questions came around to the purpose of the Home and the nature of its occupants. What were the girls like? Had they committed any crimes? Were they likely to commit any?

"I'll answer those questions a little later, if I may," Benton said. He was having a hard time getting his thoughts together. On the way over to the castle, Walter Hoving had advised him, "Go easy, John—some of these people may not know what you mean when you talk about the Lord. Remember, you're not at a prayer meeting." Trying to answer the questions without mentioning Jesus Christ was impossible. Benton felt tongue-tied.

A man in the back of the room stood up to speak. "Mr. Benton, I guess most of us have read about the kind of place you have over there. Isn't it like any other rehabilitation center?"

Benton hesitated. "Not really," he said, looking at Elsie. *Here we go again,* his expression said.

"It's not like Synanon or Daytop or Lexington?" the man persisted.

Benton shook his head. "No. In some respects we may be alike—but not in all."

"Well, maybe it would help us to understand if you would explain things," the man said, and some of those around him nodded. "What *is* the difference?"

Walter Hoving stood up, his gentle blue eyes suddenly intent. "Let me answer that, John," he said. He looked from one side of the room to the other, as if to let everyone see that he meant his words for each one directly.

"The difference in this Home is Jesus Christ!" he said in a low voice that carried clearly out to the hallway, where the late arrivals were standing. "Jesus Christ is in the very walls of that house."

Oh-oh, Benton thought, and wondered whether he ought to reman standing or sit down. *And I was the one who was supposed to remember we weren't at a prayer meeting!*

"There isn't much that you or I or anyone else can do to help these girls," Hoving said. "Don't think a lot of people haven't tried. Some of them come from good homes, from parents who did their best to bring them up the right way. Some of them have been to other rehabilitation centers. They've had the best care that private and tax money could offer them—and still it didn't help!

"Do you want to know why?" he challenged. "Because only Jesus Christ has the power to change a life, to wipe out the sins of the past, so a girl or a boy can start a new existence.

"Now, I'm not saying these girls can't find Jesus Christ in some place other than Garrison, New York. Of course they can! But the fact is, he's already in that Home, so why should they have to start all over again somewhere else?" Hoving sat down. He was matter-of-fact, not angry. "Sorry I interrupted you, John," he said. "Please go on."

In spite of the pressure, Benton smiled. Walter Hoving had said it all, and Benton was grateful.

"Ladies and gentlemen—neighbors, and, I hope friends—" he said, "I'd like to introduce two young women who have been sitting here very nervously for the past half hour. They won't keep you long, and they asked me to limit their time to five minutes each." He turned to the two girls and nodded, indicating that they should stand and face the group. The girls stood.

Benton reached out to the tall, athletic-looking girl with straight black hair that came to her shoulders. "This is Maria Hunt, and we're very proud of her."

As the other girl took her seat, Maria grasped John Benton's hand and allowed him to lead her to the front of the room. He moved off to the side as she began to speak.

She was nervous and spoke rapidly, looking over the heads of her audience. It was a story of pain, of misunderstanding and bitterness. Maria's parents had been divorced when she was five years old. She had two older sisters. Her mother worked and her father helped pay for the children's support, but money was always short. The family lived in the ghetto, and although Maria's mother tried to give her children a Christian upbringing, she was away from home most of the time. She had no antidote for the poisonous atmosphere of the ghetto streets, and in time her children were infected.

"I was never on drugs," Maria said. "I stole things. I got into other kinds of trouble—immoral things." She paused and bit her lip, refusing to cry. "My family is proud. They are decent people. It hurt them very much, but I didn't see that then.

"I've been in jail. Several times. My family thought it might scare me into changing. But it didn't. It just showed me that there are lots of other people like me."

A social worker told Maria's mother about Teen Challenge and The Walter Hoving Home. To Maria it seemed better than jail, and she agreed to go there if they would have her.

Maria took a deep breath and closed her eyes. When she opened them she looked directly into the faces in front of her.

"That's the bad news," she said, smiling for the first time. "Now let me give you the good news." Her speech changed. She spoke more slowly, obviously enjoying the memory of what she described.

"I had heard my mother talk about God and about God's love, but I never felt it. *How could God love me?* I used to think. Well, he does. He loves me very much. I was nothing, but he made me into something. Whatever I've been is finished, wiped clean.

"Sure, sometimes I get depressed. Sometimes the old temptations are very strong. But there's a difference between being tempted and giving in to it—Jesus taught me that. I hold onto him until the depression passes and I'm safe again. In the Bible it says, 'The word of the Lord creates purity within yourself,' and I have found that to be true.

"I'm new. I'm pure and I'm free. I want to go to school, and I want to learn, and I want to help other people find the freedom I found."

Maria sat down and bowed her head.

For a moment no one spoke. A few people cleared their throats. Then John Benton held out his hand to the other girl, a round-faced, pretty blonde who brushed her bangs away from her forehead before she spoke.

"My name is Diane Scott," she said. "I lived with my family in the suburbs. We had a lovely house. My father had a good job. I was an only child, and my parents fussed over me a lot. They especially wanted me to get good grades in school and go on to college. That was very important to them.

"I did very well in school most of the time. Then one day I got my report card and I had a C in one of my courses. In my family that would have been as bad as failing. I didn't know what to do, but I sure didn't want to go home. I was in the girls' room, crying, when one of my friends came in. She told me how I could solve my problem. She helped me change the C to an A.

"It worked. My parents never knew the difference, and they signed the card. Then, when I took it back to school, my friend changed the A back to a C.

"I never realized it would be so easy to lie. I was very excited about it. That meant I didn't have to work so hard in school. I could do as I pleased and tell my parents anything they wanted to hear. And that's what I did.

"I started to smoke and drink. Then I went on to pot

and speed. My friends were the people who did those things, too.

"By the time my family found out what I was doing, I didn't care what they thought. I dared them to do something about the way I lived. I dared them to throw me out. They never did. I realize now that they loved me too much to do that, but then I didn't understand. I thought they were stupid."

Diane heard of the Home from a friend, a girl who had been there. Diane had seen the girl at parties and then she didn't see her for a long time. When they met again, Diane couldn't believe it was the same girl. "She looked so fresh, so beautiful, so happy. Suddenly I was afraid to look at myself in the mirror, but I made myself do it.

"I was a mess. I was only nineteen, and I looked fifty. A sick fifty. I had dark circles under my eyes, and my skin was grayish. My hair was stringy and dirty. I don't know why I didn't see those things until that day—I mean, I looked at myself in the mirror every day, but I must have been blind most of the time.

"I was scared. I didn't want to look like that. I didn't want to *be* like that. I wanted to be like that other girl."

Diane smiled shyly. "Now I *am* like that other girl—and I don't have to look in a mirror to know it. I feel new inside. God knows all there is to know about me, and yet he loves me. I see his love in the people at the Home—I see it in the other girls—I see it in my parents.

"There isn't any point in lying—I understand that now. I can tell the truth about who and what I am and know that people will forgive me if I did something wrong. And even if some people can't forgive me, God can. He already has. So when I become afraid that somebody isn't going to like me—when I think I'm going to be rejected—I remind myself how much God loves me. That's enough. That's everything!"

Diane smiled at Elsie Benton and sat down next to Maria. The girls clasped each other's hands.

The room was very quiet. *Really, what can anyone say?* Marian Osborn thought.

Perry Osborn stood up. "If anyone has any questions—" He stopped. Several men and women had reached for their handkerchiefs. Perry looked at John Benton.

"A few minutes ago I postponed my answers to some of your questions," John Benton said. "I thought the girls could answer them better than I could. And they did. But if you have any more—" A few people shook their heads.

Marian Osborn headed toward the hallway. "As I mentioned, there will be some refreshments," she said, smiling. "Why don't we all just move to the room across the hall where we can relax and be more neighborly."

The Certificate of Occupancy did not come up for approval for some time, but when it did, the vote was a unanimous 5 to 0 in favor of approval.

CHAPTER 7

A lot had happened to the Home in the nine years since it became part of the Garrison community. Large as the three-story house seemed at first, it became crowded with more staff members and many more girls. Even Elsie Benton felt the squeeze.

"Living in one room is beginning to get to me," she said to her husband one day. "We really don't have a home at all." She didn't want to complain, but she knew it was better to admit her discomfort.

"What do you mean, 'one room'?" John teased her. He swept his arm in front of him. "You've got a whole house!"

"No, I don't. And neither do you. Each of us needs a place where we can get off by ourselves—to think, to pray, to be a family. Our room is so crowded, I can't even find a place to sit down."

"I know, honey. But first things first—and at the moment we aren't first. It takes a lot of money to build a house, even a small one, and right now we need more room for the girls."

Elsie knew he was right. Given a choice, she would have lived in one room for the rest of her life rather than turn away a girl who wanted to come to the Home.

Benton, the reluctant administrator, budgeted carefully. He also began sending out a monthly newsletter to churches, former contributors, and businesses whose executives had expressed interest in the Home's program. Walter Hoving gave him more names to contact. As some of the girls went through the program and graduated, Benton was able to begin quoting statistics, and that helped. "Miracles are happening," he told people when he asked them to help support the Home. "Nine out of ten girls who finish the program remain cured." If anybody wanted proof, he had a list of graduates in his desk drawer. He knew where the girls were and what they were doing. Sometimes, when he wondered how the Home would survive another crisis, he took out the list and read through it. It was amazing what those girls had done with their lives! No—it was amazing what *God* had done.

Some of the girls still came back to visit the Home. A few joined the staff after graduating from Bible school. Many of them went on to work in Teen Challenge centers. Benton could understand why. These girls understood what it was to be on the bottom of the world. They knew, better than anyone else, how to reach out and help someone else get up from the bottom, and to them it was the most meaningful way they could celebrate their new life. Benton learned a lot from them.

Slowly the money came in. In August of each year, when most people took their vacations, times were hard, but during the Christmas season the donations were especially generous. Finally, in the fall of 1973, the Home had enough money to begin construction on a new dormitory. It was finished the next summer, and once again there were more rooms. The next year, when Sandy McKay arrived in the middle of a snowstorm, there were twenty-five girls living at the Home.

Poor Sandy, Elsie thought as she drove away from the gas station where Sandy's car was being repaired. It had taken a lot of courage for her to come to the Home. Elsie had wanted to plead with her to stay a little longer, but she knew better than to try. Much as it pained her to see Sandy leave, Elsie had lived through enough agonies with enough girls to realize that, crippling as their destructive way of life may have been, that was all they had. Giving up something familiar in exchange for ways that were unknown, untried, was terrifying. "Walking the plank," one girl had called it. "You just don't know what you're going to fall into," she had said.

Change took time. It didn't happen immediately, and it hurt when it did happen. In the meantime, what was a girl to hang onto? In a sense, Elsie decided, a girl had to have faith almost before she knew what faith was. But that was what faith was all about, and that was the way it had to happen. God didn't take shortcuts.

Elsie didn't doubt God's wisdom. Some people thought that the girls who came to the Home were cured by "finding Christ." Well, it wasn't that simple. Lots of people "found" Christ, shook hands with him, and went on their way as if nothing had happened. And nothing *did* happen. A lot of girls gave up on the Home because they weren't able to take the next step and give their lives to Christ, completely and without holding anything back. Commitment meant trying to live his way twenty-four hours a day, forever. *He* made the decisions, *he* told you when you were right and when you were wrong—hardly a simple procedure. Elsie knew that even when a girl wanted to give her life to Christ, she gave it up an inch at a time, and always after a struggle. Only when that last inch was surrendered did she realize that she was finally free from her own destructive nature. That's when a girl began saying things like "Praise the Lord!" and "Hallelujah!" because she knew no better words to express her joy. She was in good hands, at last.

There were so many Sandys in the world. Some of them came back to the Home and tried again. Some of them—well, Elsie hated to think about what happened to some of them.

The chains on the tires bit into the snow in the driveway as Elsie pulled the car around to the parking area in front of the house. Turning off the ignition, she leaned back in her seat to rest a moment after the strain of driving on slippery roads. Her back ached from the tension in her muscles. In the rear-view mirror she saw someone passing behind the car, walking in the direction of the dormitory. Realizing who it was, she smiled. Only one of the girls would be dressed so properly. It had to be Sue. Everyone else wore jeans or old wool pants and anything else that kept a person warm on such a day, but Sue wore well-pressed gray tweed pants and a matching jacket. A blue-and-white knitted cap covered almost all of her soft, wavy brown hair, and Elsie saw that her mittens matched the cap. Sue was so correct, so unbending. Elsie thought she would rather die than put on a pair of jeans.

But that was the trouble with Sue. She wouldn't let down her guard. She was one of those who had found Christ and couldn't seem to go any farther. Some of the girls said Sue thought she was better than the rest of them, but Elsie didn't agree. If anything, Sue kept her distance because she didn't want anyone—not even God—to know what a terrible person she was.

Sue had seen Elsie sitting in the car and kept her head down against the cold because she didn't want to wave. Mom B—as the girls called Mrs. Benton—might get out of the car, which meant Sue would have to stop and talk to her. Sue didn't want that. This was one of the days when she couldn't stand Mom B. She didn't want anyone hugging her and telling her that she ought to try to relax.

Relax! That would have been the end of everything. Sue was proud of her self-control. She had worked at it ever since she could remember, and without it she would have come apart. She knew. It had happened. But it wasn't going to happen again. That was why she had come to the Home—to learn how to increase her control over herself.

At the entrance to the dorm Sue kicked the snow from her boots lightly. She disapproved of the way most of the girls stomped on the doormat, and looked around to see if anyone noticed the example she was setting. The only person she saw was Mom B getting out of the car. Turning quickly, Sue went inside and up the stairs to the room she shared with three other girls. At the moment the room was empty, which pleased her. She took off her jacket, hung it in the closet, and lay down on her bed.

The room wasn't so bad, really. The two double-tiered bunk beds were made of light-stained wood, and the mattresses were comfortable. The walls looked as if they had just been painted white, and the carpet was soft and clean. Yes, it was all very new and clean, which Sue liked. She just objected to the lack of privacy. The only way she could spend some time alone was to eat her meals quickly and get back to her room before her roommates did.

Oh, well, she had had worse, much worse.

She turned over and lay face down. She didn't want to

remember, but lately she couldn't help it. How she hated going back—to the little New England town where she was born and where her mother died when Sue was four years old. The memory always began as a blur of adult voices speaking quietly, stopping their conversation when she wandered into the room where people were deciding what to do with her. Her father was unable to run his farm alone and care for Sue and her five brothers and sisters. He intended to look for work in another town. The children would have to be placed in an orphanage—only temporarily, until he got on his feet.

Temporarily—Sue still winced at the word. She and her brothers and sisters spent five years in the orphanage. They were separated from each other from the day they entered because the supervisors thought it would be easier to control them if they were not together. Now and then, when Sue caught a glimpse of her brothers and sisters, she ran toward them, screaming. Hands, strong hands, caught her and held her back.

Young as she was, Sue began making a decision that was to shape her life. She would not allow herself to cry or to express pain. She would become a model inmate and avoid friction, not because she wanted to please, but because she did not want to kill. The anger she felt when she was held back from the only people she knew and loved was more than she could handle. If provoked, she was afraid it might destroy her along with everyone else. The only solution was to hide her anger beneath a gentle voice, a shy manner, and a sweet smile.

When Sue's father got back on his feet, he remarried. Neither he nor his wife wanted to take on the responsibilities of a family, and since he had not seen his children often enough to strengthen his fatherly feelings, he asked the orphanage to find foster homes for them.

According to the orphanage, Sue was lucky. She remained with the same family until she was seventeen. Her brothers and sisters were moved from home to home, never feeling that they belonged anywhere. As soon as they were old enough, they went off on their own and lost contact with each other.

According to Sue, however, she was miserable. Her foster parents, hard-working farmers, were uncomfortable with a child in their home. They had no children of their own, no one with whom they could compare the behavior of the sweet-faced little girl they had agreed to bring up. Every move Sue made was suspect, each mistake was a sin of monstrous size. Yet she was a good child. As far as she was able, she did as she was told, never complaining when she was instructed to "come straight home from school after class" and help with the work on the farm. She had no friends–she had no time to make any. Laughing and talking with other girls was called "a waste of time," and being in the company of a boy was "wicked." Once, when she was sixteen and a boy walked her home from school, Sue's foster mother said, "You're a tramp!"

"No!" Sue protested. "It was nothing like that! He didn't even hold my hand."

"What do you mean, 'nothing like that'?" her foster mother said, stepping away from her. "You know too much for a girl your age!"

"I'm sixteen," Sue said. "I'm not a baby."

"No, indeed. I was right–you're a tramp!"

From that day Sue was watched more carefully than ever. *It must be true,* she thought. *I'm a tramp.*

Sue did well in school. At first she worked hard to get the kind of grades that would improve her standing with her foster parents. When they were unimpressed, partly because they placed little value on time spent in a classroom, she worked even harder, convinced that an education would help her achieve the one thing in the world she wanted: her independence. She counted the months, the weeks, and the days until her eighteenth birthday.

Most of Sue's teachers liked her. How could they help it? She was so agreeable, so well-behaved. During her junior year, Frank Holiday, her English teacher, was especially encouraging. When he saw how quickly she read the books assigned to the class, he brought her more books from his own library. If only she could have lingered after school and talked to him about them. *One more year to go,* she reminded herself, *and then I can do as I please.*

But it was less than a year before her life changed completely. Her foster parents were ill, and the farm, which had never been a moneymaker, had to be sold. They were going to move in with relatives, and there would be no room for Sue. The orphanage would find another foster home for her—it would be for such a short time.

When Frank Holiday learned that he was about to lose his most promising student, he couldn't accept it. He told his wife, Betty, about the quiet, subdued young girl who had such a hunger to learn, and she agreed that they should try to help. The Holidays had two young children—if Sue came to live with them, she could help take care of them.

"Maybe you ought to meet the girl first," Frank suggested. "You don't even know what she's like, and I don't want you to be sorry."

"No," Betty said, putting her arms around him. "I'll take your word for her."

Suddenly Sue had the freedom she wanted, and it was too much for her. The Holidays trusted her completely. They wanted her to have friends and catch up on all the good times she had missed. She came home from school whenever she pleased, and no questions were asked. She helped Betty with the housework on Saturdays and sometimes sat with the children. On Sunday she attended church services with the Holidays, as if she were one of the family. She was loved and encouraged and respected so much that she let down her guard. She no longer seemed to need such rigid self-control.

Sue remembered the exact moment when she relaxed her grip on herself. She was at home with three-year-old Jeannie, the Holidays' little girl. Frank, Betty, and their six-year-old son, Billy, were at the circus. She and Jeannie were on the bed in Sue's room, playing paddy-cake.

As Sue clapped her hands and placed them gently against Jeannie's upraised hands, counting out the rhythm, the child giggled delightedly. *What a wonderful life this child has!* Sue thought. *No one ever played paddy-cake with me when I was her age.* Ordinarily she would have censored such resentment, but this time she allowed it to consume her.

Paddy-cake, paddy-cake, baker's man,
Bake your cake as fast as you can. . . .

Now, as Sue reached out to place her hands against Jeannie's, Sue began to push, harder and harder each time, until finally the child fell over backward. Surprised, she looked at Sue inquiringly.

Paddy-cake was over. Sue leaned over the child and put her hands around the tiny waist. She began pressing, pressing, as if she wanted to squeeze the life out of Jeannie's body. Frightened, Jeannie began to cry, and Sue realized that she was pleased at the sound. She *wanted* to hurt this adored, sheltered, nourished child as much as she had been hurt—even more! She wanted to kill her.

Downstairs there were voices. The Holidays were home

and Billy was running up the stairs, looking for Sue so he could tell her about the wonderful things he had seen at the circus. Quickly, Sue released her grip on Jeannie and began to tickle the child, forcing herself to laugh playfully as the child squirmed to be free of her. As Billy came in, Sue held Jeannie close to her and kissed her, smoothing her damp, blond hair away from her forehead. She felt the child beginning to relax in her arms and knew she would soon forget what happened. She was too young to understand.

But something was out of its cage. Every hurt, every slight and humiliation Sue had ever known came forth, insisting that the score must be settled. And why not? She was free to collect the debts that were owed her.

It was Sue's senior year in high school and she decided that catching up on fun was not enough. Her foster mother had called her a tramp. Well, she would be one! No more basketball games and meetings after school—there were better things to do if you knew the right people. And Sue got to know the right people. They convinced her that a party was more fun if she got drunk, that marijuana would calm her nerves, and that stealing what she wanted was more exciting than buying it. They taught her that sex was a matter of convenience, and that lying was a triumph of intelligence over stupidity.

The Holidays never knew. Sometimes, when Sue sat curled up in one of the living-room chairs, she pretended to be reading, but actually she was watching Frank and Betty for signs of suspicion. There were none. They accepted Sue for what she seemed to be on the surface—a pretty, although somewhat plain girl, who, given half a chance, would grow up to be a fine young woman. They were amazed at her lack of bitterness at all the deprivations in her life.

Sometimes the Holidays became concerned about the hours Sue kept. Even on weeknights she rarely was home before midnight. But they were reluctant to question her about where she had been or what she had done—Sue had had so much of that already.

"Let her be," Frank said when Betty told him she thought Sue had been drinking one night. "She'll settle down. It's just something she's going through."

"I suppose so," Betty said, but she was troubled. "She isn't keeping up with her schoolwork, you know. It's bound to affect her grades."

"Maybe that's what she needs—a little scare. She'll pull out of it."

Sue's grades were worse than she expected. She was on the verge of failing. But she was more practical than afraid; she still needed that high-school diploma. For the last semester of her senior year she did her homework before she went out at night.

The Holidays were shocked when they went to Sue's graduation and Sue wasn't there. They came home to find that she had packed her clothes in two of their suitcases and gone. She left a note in which she thanked them—formally and briefly—for all they had done, including the gift of the two suitcases which, she assumed, they would have wanted her to have. She was eighteen now and on her own. Goodbye.

CHAPTER 8

Sue liked Boston better than the small towns she had lived in since she left the Holidays. She could make more money in a big city, and money was very important to her. She was a good typist and took shorthand, so it was easy for her to get a job in an office. At night she worked as a waitress in a restaurant near the room she rented. She had more money than she ever knew existed, and still it was not enough. She spent most of it on clothes. They were good clothes, she reassured herself whenever she was down to her last dollar before payday, not the cheap hand-me-downs she had worn all her life. Sometimes she changed her mind about a blouse or a skirt she had bought and threw it away without even wearing it. That, to her, was freedom.

She had very few friends. She didn't like most of the girls she met at work. She considered them silly and beneath her intellectually. Once she had taken in a roommate, a girl who worked in an office down the hall from her, but she didn't like the way the girl was always trying to be helpful. Sue didn't need a mother.

Men were attracted to Sue. She had known that since her senior year in high school, and while the discovery surprised her then, she now took it for granted. She was not a beauty. She was neat, well-scrubbed and healthy-looking, but that was all, and she knew it. In fact, she reveled in it. When she needed glasses, she chose the plainest silver-rimmed frames she could find. *I dare you to love me*, she was saying. And men did—at least a certain kind of man. Sue's shy, soft-spoken manner appealed to men who wanted to protect a helpless young girl who had had some bad breaks in life. All she needed was a few moments' conversation with the right kind of man and she could do anything she liked with him. She enjoyed playing games, but only for a while, because she never felt anything for any man she had ever met. No, that wasn't true, she had to admit. She was afraid of men, afraid they would eventually go off and leave her, just as her father had done. She never gave a man a chance to say goodbye. She was the one who said it first.

Meeting men was never a problem. There were lots of lonely men—most of them married—who came to the restaurant where she worked. Sometimes, late at night, she went to a bar, but the men she met there weren't as eager to protect her. Except for Don Bellows. He was different.

He was tall and muscular, with brown hair graying at the temples. He wore glasses and dressed very well, always in a business suit. He seemed friendly and lonely and far from home, a combination that usually worked well for Sue. She enjoyed talking to him. He said he was in the import business and would be in Boston for a few months. Don always had a lot of money, and Sue was flattered because he spent so much of it on her.

"Your business must be very successful," she said to him one night.

He smiled as if she had told a joke. "Sometimes," he said, and changed the subject.

Then he was gone. He left without telling her. He simply didn't pick her up at the restaurant one night. He didn't phone or write from wherever he was, and Sue was furious. He had fooled her. *She* was the one who should have disappeared.

A month later Sue opened the door of her apartment to find a young, good-looking man grinning at her.

"Let me in, honey," he said, pushing against the door.

"No, you don't!" Sue said, throwing herself against the door. She was too frightened to scream.

He was inside. He slammed the door and leaned against it, laughing. "You don't remember me?" he said.

As she realized he was not going to harm her, she studied his face. Who was he? In a way he looked like—

"Don!" she said. The gray was gone from his hair, and there were no glasses. Instead of a business suit he wore a knitted shirt and jeans. But it was Don Bellows.

"Contact lenses," he said. "And a little hair dye. Makes all the difference, right?"

He was lying. The glasses, the distinguished gray hair, the conservative clothes—*they* were the disguise. The person she saw now was the real Don Bellows. He looked ten years younger, but there also was a strange excitement about him, a presence of danger. Far from feeling threatened by it, she was attracted to it.

"Where were you?" she said, as he put his arms around her.

"Mexico," he said. "It's nice there—you'd like it." He stroked her hair.

"How long are you going to stay this time?" she asked.

"That depends on you."

Sue pulled away from him. "That's why you're here, isn't it? You want something!" Once again he had fooled her.

"That's right," he said, and the confidence in his grin

infuriated her. He sat down in the large wing chair, the only comfortable chair in the room. "I need a place to stay."

"Well, not here!"

"You don't understand, Susie. I'm hiding from the police, so I can't very well check into a hotel."

"The police? Why? What have you done?"

"I robbed a bank," he said. He looked at her steadily, waiting for her reaction.

Sue's expression revealed nothing. "Did you use a gun?" she said.

"I did," he said.

"Is that what you really are? A bank robber?"

"More or less. Does that bother you?"

Shrieking like a child, she threw herself into his lap and curled up against him. "It makes me extremely happy!" she whispered.

He laughed. "I was right about you, wasn't I? You only *look* innocent."

She enjoyed the compliment and sat up smugly. "I don't know what I am—but I like excitement. I especially like to do what everybody tells you not to do."

"Like robbing banks?"

She nodded. "And using a gun. Will you teach me how?"

"Do I have a place to stay?"

She nodded.

He was serious now. He offered her his hand. "Deal? Partners?"

She shook hands. "Partners."

At first Sue gave up her job at the restaurant so she could spend her evenings with Don. Then, when it seemed that Don had plenty of money for both of them, she called the office where she worked and told her boss she wasn't coming in anymore. She had better things to do.

Gradually, and with great caution, Don moved his arsenal of weapons into Sue's room and stored them carefully in the back of her large closet. There were several handguns, a shotgun with the barrel sawed off, and two rifles, one with a scope. He had boxes of ammunition, plus a small canister of tear gas.

The guns fascinated Sue. She loved to hold one in her hand and aim it at objects in the room. Don got nervous when she aimed it at him.

"It isn't loaded," she said.

"I know," he said. "It's just the look on your face that scares me. You really want to use that thing, don't you?"

"Of course," she said, putting the gun in her lap. "Don't you?"

He shook his head. "You know, I've never pulled the trigger—except to practice."

"That's silly!" she said. "Why do you carry a gun if you're not going to use it?"

"I don't have to. The sight of the gun gets me what I want. But with you it's different, isn't it? You really want to shoot somebody?"

"Maybe," she said. She was uncomfortable because he was afraid of her. It might be a sign of weakness in him.

"When are you going to teach me how to use a gun?" she asked.

"Soon. We're running out of money, which means we have to go back to work."

"A bank?"

"Right."

"Oh, Don, that's wonderful!" she said, throwing her arms around him "When?"

"Next week."

Sue never got to rob a bank. She went with Don to a small bank on a busy corner and spent her days standing across the street from the building, watching as customers came and went, determining which hours were quiet and when the traffic was light. But two days before the robbery, Don was recognized and picked up by the police.

When two detectives came to her room to question her about Don, she remembered his instructions. She pretended to be shocked at learning he was a criminal, and she knew she was convincing. Who would ever suspect anything else? She knew how she looked. If only they didn't search her room. They didn't.

Don wasn't taking any chances. He wanted to get rid of his weapons, and when Sue went to visit him in the county jail he told her to take them to a friend, who would know what to do with them.

"But do it at night, the way I did. One at a time," he warned.

"Why?" she asked him. "Why not do something better with the guns, or at least one of them?"

He glanced over his shoulder toward the guard at the door, who was looking in another direction. "You mean you want to smuggle a gun in here, don't you?"

She smiled and nodded. "I can, too. You know I can."

"With that face, you can," he said, leaning toward her.

To anyone watching them, they appeared to be talking about ordinary things, or perhaps about Don's defense. The girl seemed too nice to be mixed up with that kind of a man, but maybe she wasn't very smart. You never could tell.

Actually Sue and Don were planning a jailbreak. Sue

would smuggle in a gun and leave a rented car parked outside. It would be easy, Sue assured him. She had noticed that there were hardly any security precautions at the jail. She never was searched. Only her handbag was opened and the contents examined. She could do it!

The next day she rented a car in the morning and parked it behind the jail. She left the keys in the ignition. Then she went inside. She had taped one of the pistols to the inside of her left thigh, but no one noticed that she was walking somewhat stiffly, because she had practiced for hours the night before. Her stride was almost normal, especially to anyone who didn't know her well.

She was wearing a full skirt, and during her visit with Don she was able to reach under it and untape the gun without attracting the guard's attention. She slipped the gun to Don. To avoid suspicion, she visited for over an hour. The rest was up to Don.

Leaving the jail, she walked down the street to a small park between two tall buildings. She sat on a bench, waiting. Twenty minutes later, the rented car went by so fast she almost missed seeing it. She had never been so excited! In a few days Don would let her know where he was, and they could be together again.

Outside Sue's room the same two detectives were waiting for her. They had put two and two together, and this time they had a warrant to search her room, and a warrant for her arrest. Don had been caught before he got out of the city.

The detectives were sarcastic. Now she could spend all her time in jail, they said, as they took her downstairs to their car.

When Sue was sentenced to one year in a correctional home for women, she shrugged.

"It's just as well," she told the public defender who had

handled her case. "Jobs aren't so easy to get right now. At least I'll have room and board in prison."

The young lawyer shook his head sadly. He thought Sue was trying to act hard. She wasn't. Prison was a tremendous relief to her. She had never been so comfortable in her life. There was very little work for the inmates to do, and most of the time Sue slept. She got up only to eat and walk in the courtyard, her only form of exercise. She was putting on weight, but she didn't care. The hatred deep inside her had taken command of her life, and she welcomed it. She no longer had to pretend to be decent.

Sue's lawyer had warned her about the girls she would meet in prison, many of them in on charges far more serious than hers. "Try to keep your distance," he said. "You've got enough trouble." They could teach her the wrong kind of things.

But Sue liked most of the inmates. Some were hostile at first, but she realized they were only trying to test her reaction to them. She never let them get away with anything—and once, when a girl stole her comb, Sue attacked her with her fists, her nails, and her teeth. After that, there was no more hostility. Gradually there was friendship, an awkward kind of tenderness that came from the girls' understanding that they were alike. They were together in a bad situation, which gave Sue a feeling that she was part of a family. She had never felt that way before. Always she had been the outsider, unwanted or pitied. She was the different one, her feelings too alien to be shared by others in the homes that had sheltered her. Here, in prison, she realized that there were others like her. They may have been garbage—which was Sue's description of herself—but they were all in the same trash can.

At night, before the final bedtime count of the inmates, Sue and several other girls in the crowded twenty-bed dormitory where she slept sat around her bunk bed and listened to a radio, switching to another station whenever the news report came on. Some of the girls were eager to finish their sentence and leave, but even they wanted nothing to do with the outside world. Not yet.

To Sue the thought of parole was threatening. It meant she had to try to slip back into her old act again—the sweet, innocent young girl who couldn't possibly do anything wrong. How she hated that part of herself—and along with it she hated anyone who believed the lie. They were the real phonies in this world! People like the Holidays didn't want to know who she really was. They were more comfortable with the counterfeit she offered.

There was a reason why most of the girls tried to avoid talking about the outside world and the future: It hurt too much. But when one of the girls was about to be released, the others forgot the wounds of past experiences and began to speculate.

"What are you going to do when you're out, Debbie?" Sue asked the girl who had become her closest friend. Debbie had been granted a parole and was to leave the next day.

"You won't believe me if I tell you," Debbie said, curling her arms around her knees and looking away.

"Why not?"

"You'll think I'm crazy—and maybe I am."

Sue poked her in the ribs playfully. "Okay, you're crazy. I don't care. Tell me." The other girls were quiet, waiting for Debbie's answer.

"Okay," Debbie said. She sat up very straight, ready to defend herself against ridicule. "I'm going to go to church."

Somebody giggled, and Debbie glared in the girl's direction.

Sue was shocked. "You're kidding!"

Debbie shook her head. She was serious.

"You mean that's all you're going to do? Just go to church?" Sue said.

"No, stupid! You can't make a living going to church. Anyway, I'm not worried about getting a job—I'll do something. But there's a church in my neighborhood—I went there a few times after the pastor came around to see me. He was a nice old man—really made me feel that people wanted me there. And they did. I walked up to the front door a couple of Sundays in a row and then turned right around and went home—I didn't have the nerve to go in at first. When I did, I was glad. They were nice people."

"I know," Sue said, remembering the Sunday morning services with the Holidays. "I went to church for a while, too."

"Well, this old minister has been coming to see me every now and then."

"Here?"

"Here. He just keeps saying the same thing—that I ought to come to church when I get out. It doesn't seem to make any difference that I'm in here." Debbie stood up. "So that's what I'm going to do." She smiled at Sue. "See, I knew you'd think I was crazy!"

"But *why?* I don't understand. Why?"

"Look I don't feel the way you do about this place," Debbie said, sitting down again. "This is my second time, and I don't want to spend the rest of my life here. I think there may be something else for me—I don't know what. I don't know how. But maybe this church can help me find out. It's worth trying." She reached over and mussed Sue's hair. "Don't worry. It probably won't work, and I'll be back here before you get out.

"Anyway, I'm leaving you my radio," she said, standing up again.

"Hey, thanks."

"That's so you won't forget me."

Suddenly Sue felt as if she were going to cry. "I'll never do that," she mumbled, fighting her tears. Now she realized how much it hurt to see one of the girls leave. She was happy for Debbie, because parole was what Debbie wanted, but she would miss her friend. And with the realization that Debbie was leaving came the awareness that she too must one day face the question of what she was going to do once she got out.

"Don't worry your head about things like that," said Gloria, the girl in the bunk next to hers. "I've been through it, so I can tell you. You know what you'll do? The same old thing! You'll swear you won't be so dumb and you won't get caught again, but they'll get you. You'll meet up with the same kind of guy and make the same mistakes." She grinned and looked around at the other girls. "Right?" she asked. They nodded and murmured agreement.

Oh, well, Sue thought, *I'm luckier than most. I like it here.*

CHAPTER 9

"Sue, you have a visitor," the matron said.

Sue was puzzled. No one ever came to see her. No one knew where she was.

The visitors' room was crowded and hazy with smoke. The faces she saw were unfamiliar, until suddenly she recognized Betty Holiday.

"How did you find me?" Sue said.

"We had to ask a lot of people," Betty said. She threw her arms around Sue. "Oh, Sue, you poor baby!"

Gently, Sue pulled herself free. "Why don't we sit down," she said.

"Frank and I think about you all the time," Betty said. "Every night we pray for you—the children, too. They're getting so big, you wouldn't know them." There were tears in her pale blue eyes, and she swallowed hard.

Sue was so surprised by the visit that she could think of nothing to say. She was embarrassed by Betty's presence—how could the woman sit there as if nothing had happened?

"Sue, the other night we were talking about you, and—well, Frank and I would like you to come to stay with us when—when—" She groped for words.

"When I get out?" Sue said. Betty's clumsiness amused her.

"Yes, when you get out. You'll need a place to live, for a while at least, until you know what you want to do."

Sue wanted to hurt her. "Does this mean you also want your two suitcases back?" she said softly.

"Sue!"

"If that's what you want, you're out of luck. I lost them."

Betty grasped Sue's hands. "Sue, you don't understand. We love you! That's why we want you to stay with us. We don't care about those old suitcases."

"No, *you* don't understand! It makes you feel good to say you love me, but you really don't. You couldn't—not if you knew what I am." She held up her hand when Betty tried to interrupt.

"Do you know that I used you and Frank? That I *made* you feel sorry for me—I made Frank feel sorry for me before I even knew you! All those books I used to borrow—I did it to get his attention, to make him feel guilty if he wasn't nice to me."

Betty was crying. She covered her face with her hands.

For a moment Sue regretted what she had done. The unexpected surge of sympathy was uncomfortable. "I tried to kill your little girl!" she said, raising her voice, not caring who heard her. Betty stared at her.

"I lied to you and you loved it! You didn't want to know how rotten I was, so I almost killed Jeannie to make you understand. The day you and Frank took Billy to the circus—you came home just in time!"

"I don't believe it!" Betty whispered.

"Oh, yes, you do. You don't want to, but you're beginning to believe it. You're beginning to see what I am. I lie, I steal, I hurt people—and I might even kill. Now—do you still want me to come to live with you?"

Betty hung her head. The tears rolled down her cheeks and into her lap where her hands were clenched. "I don't know," she said. "I wouldn't be honest if I said 'Yes' at this moment." She took a deep breath and looked at Sue. "Frank and I have to think about this. We have to pray about it." Then she remembered something.

"I left a package with the matron. It's your graduation present—a little late." She was sobbing now, and she ran to the door. The matron let her out.

Sue went back to her dormitory, carrying the neatly wrapped package. Somehow her triumph over Betty was disturbing. She had wanted to expose the Holidays as the hypocrites she knew they had to be. She wanted to make Betty say, "No, we don't want you!" Why didn't she say it? *Give her time,* Sue decided. *Give her time. Tomorrow she'll wish she had said it!*

She threw the package onto her bed, wishing she could throw it away without opening it. But she couldn't. She sat staring at it for a long time. Then she picked it up and tore at the string and the brown paper wrapping. Inside a plain cream-colored box was a white leather Bible with her name printed in gold on the cover.

First Debbie. Now this. It was a conspiracy. She tossed the Bible across the bed and reached around to turn on her radio. It was gone.

"Who took it?" she screamed, climbing up on a wooden chair next to her bed and looking around the room. About half the girls were there. "Who took my radio?"

"Whoever it was, I'll kill her!" Sue shouted.

When no one answered she got off the chair and picked it up. Smashing it against the concrete floor until it broke into pieces, she seized one of the legs and held it up. "Tell me who it is—or I'll kill every one of you!"

Two matrons came up behind her and forced her arms down. Their fingers bit into her muscles and made her cry out in pain. She dropped the chair leg and tried to twist free, but they were too strong for her. She felt them pressing her forward onto the bed until she lay face down on it. And there she lay, swearing, panting, crying and threatening, while they held her down. After a long, long time, when her breathing became normal and she was too exhausted to make a sound, she was taken to a small, windowless room, where she was locked in. She fell to the floor and lay there, too weak to crawl to the metal bed, the only piece of furniture in the room.

Now she began to plan her future. Now she wanted to get out. It had to be Gloria who had taken her radio. Gloria, the girl in the bunk next to hers, who was released on parole that morning. And when Sue got out, there was only one thing she wanted to do. Get even.

Six months later Sue stood across the street from the building where Gloria was living.

"You're crazy, letting it eat away at you," the other girls had told her. "It's just a radio." But finally someone who knew Gloria gave Sue her address.

To Sue it was not "just a radio." It was a way to rid herself of the frustration she felt at the thought of getting out of jail. She would not have to go back into hiding behind the façade of sweet innocence if the façade no longer existed. By destroying Gloria, she could, at the same time, destroy that part of herself. The world would then have to reckon with the real Sue, and for her there would be no turning back.

It was a cold day in November, and she was numb from standing in one place for so long. She was waiting for Gloria to enter the building, waiting to follow her to her room. There was a row of shops where she was standing, and she pretended to look in one of the windows. She kept her hands in her pockets, and her shoulders were bunched up against the icy wind that came in sudden gusts.

When she heard someone say, "Sue?" she turned, tightening her hand around the knife in her right pocket. She hadn't considered that Gloria might see her first. That wasn't part of the plan. In the quick turning of her body she thought she might attack Gloria right there in the street, but decided it wouldn't be wise. Panic made her heart beat so hard she thought her chest would burst.

"Sue? I was right—it *is* you." The voice was familiar, and it was not Gloria's. The girl approaching her was tall and broad-shouldered. It was hard for Sue to see her face, which was nuzzled in a thick woolen scarf around her neck. She carried a small suitcase.

"It's Debbie, Sue. Don't you remember?"

Sue was shocked, not only by the unexpectedness of meeting her, but also by the change in Debbie's appearance. She had been so stoop-shouldered; her large brown eyes had been mournful, even when she smiled. The girl she saw now was straight and graceful; her eyes glowed with happiness. She put her arms around Sue and hugged her.

"You're so thin!" she said. "What happened to you? Didn't they feed you? What are you doing here? Do you live around here?" Then she laughed. "Poor Sue, all these questions."

Sue was so relieved that she couldn't speak. She held onto Debbie and felt the sting of tears in her eyes.

"I have to catch a bus," Debbie said, "but I still have a few minutes. Let's get a cup of coffee. I've got so much to tell you!"

And so it was in the steamy warmth of a luncheonette that Sue first heard about The Walter Hoving Home. The name meant nothing to her. Two minutes after Debbie mentioned it Sue couldn't remember the name. But she would remember the expression Debbie's face when she spoke about it.

"This is my first weekend away from the Home since I walked in the front door a couple of months ago," Debbie said. "And I can't believe it—I'm actually getting along with my mother!"

"Probably because you haven't seen her for so long," Sue said. She wanted to resist the pressure of Debbie's enthusiasm. She didn't like where it was taking her.

"No, it isn't that, Sue. I've changed—a lot. I feel different about people." She stirred her coffee and then looked directly into Sue's eyes. "I'm a Christian, Sue," she said. "Do you know what that means?"

"Sure. I've known a few."

Debbie ignored the cynical tone of Sue's voice. "It makes all the difference in the world when you know how much God loves you." She held up her hand to prevent Sue from speaking. "And I do mean *you*. If God can love me—and he does—well, you're a whole lot easier to love than I am."

Sue shook her head sadly. "All this religion may do something for you," she said, "but not for me. God and I haven't been on speaking terms for a long time."

Debbie looked up at the clock behind the counter. "Sue, I have to run for my bus, but I wish you were coming back to the Home with me." She pulled a paper napkin out of a dispenser on the table and took a short pencil from her handbag. Printing in large letters on the napkin, she said, "I'm writing down the address and telephone number of the Home—in case you want to use it sometime." She pushed the napkin toward Sue and got up, pulling her coat around her and picking up her suitcase.

"God bless you, Sue!" she said and kissed the top of Sue's head before she hurried out the door.

Sue ordered another cup of coffee. She didn't really want one, but it was a good excuse to sit there for a while. She had to think. It was hard to believe she had just seen the same Debbie whose bitterness had been so much like her own. If she could change—and there was no doubt in Sue's mind that she had—what did it mean to Sue?

Perhaps there was another alternative, one she had never considered. Debbie certainly wasn't pretending—she *was* different. No one could ever be that good an actress.

Change. Sue never had thought about change. Deceive or destroy—they were the only choices she had ever known.

But how? Where did a person begin? Debbie had talked about God as if he were someone she knew very well. A friend. Someone who cared about what happened to you. To Sue, God was someone—or something—vague, someone too busy with more important problems to pay attention to hers. And who was she to call his attention to her?

Garbage, she reminded herself.

She pushed the coffee away and put the napkin into her pocket, where she felt the knife, warm and smooth. She had come to do something she had planned for months, and she had wasted enough time philosophizing.

She paid the cashier and walked out into the cold. It was dark, and people were hurrying home from work. She walked back to the building where Gloria lived and went into the vestibule. She would ring someone else's bell and get in. Somehow she would find Gloria's room and surprise her. As she squinted in the dim light, trying to read the scribbled names over the mailboxes, she felt hot tears running down her face. Angrily she brushed them aside, but more followed. She couldn't read the names!

She turned around and leaned back against the mailboxes, sobbing. From her right coat pocket she pulled the knife and released the blade with a touch of her finger. Looking up, she waved the knife at the darkness. "Are you trying to tell me something, God?" she cried. "You know what I am. You know what I want to do." She jabbed the knife fiercely in the air, then let it go. It clattered on the tile floor and slid into a dirty corner.

"Oh, God!" she said, shuddering and wrapping her arms tightly around her, "thank you for stopping me."

She was still crying as she ran from the vestibule. In the pocket of her coat her fingers pressed the napkin tightly into the palm of her hand. Strangely, it felt very good.

Sue's eyes were wet with tears again. It happened every time she remembered what her life had been.

Things were very much better since she had come to the Home. Except for a few unguarded moments like this, she was regaining control over herself. Nor was she trying to pretend she was someone else. The forced sweetness was gone, but nothing else had taken its place. At times Sue simply felt dead. Oh, well, even that was better than the way she had been.

She heard footsteps on the stairs. Her roommates were coming back from the dining room. Sue turned her face to the wall and pretended to be asleep.

CHAPTER 10

If anyone understood how much Sue was suffering, it was Elsie Benton. Although Elsie's background was quite different from Sue's, she had known the pain of being unloved. Of course, that was a long time ago.

Elsie was the youngest of her parents' six children. She also was their only daughter. Perhaps it was her imagination, but from the time she was a child, she felt that she was a disappointment to her parents. She thought they wanted another boy. So she tried especially hard to be a pleasing child, to win the approval her brothers seemed to receive at their birth. Still, it eluded her.

Elsie's mother was frequently ill and spent much of her time in bed. "Elsie, make me a cup of tea, will you, dear?" Elsie could remember her mother saying. How many times a day she walked up and down the stairs bringing things to her mother, trying to satisfy her every whim the moment it was mentioned. And with every step her resentment grew. She was a good girl, but not a loved and cherished girl. Then one day she realized she was not even a good girl—not on the inside, anyway. Although it didn't show, she hated waiting on her mother and doing so much of the housework; she felt it was unfair for her brothers to have their freedom; she was jealous of her closest friends for each little attention they received from their parents.

Since she could not feel loved by others, she loved herself. She became very vain and fussed over her appearance. Her hair and her clothes had to be exactly right, and even then they did not live up to her expectations. A friend always seemed to have a prettier dress, or eyes of a color better than hers, or shoes that were more fashionable. The more attention Elsie paid to herself, the more dissatisfied she became with the results.

She was even more critical of her friends and her family. She disapproved of their manners, their way of speaking, the decisions they made. Worst of all—as she looked back—was the way she found fault with their spiritual life. At the age of seven, Elsie had walked up to the altar of her church and given her life to Jesus Christ. Not long after that she led a friend into the church and up to the altar as well. Elsie's commitment was sincere, so sincere that no one else could match it, at least not in her eyes. Wherever else she looked she found people backsliding, paying lip service to Christ. She was disappointed and also more than a little self-righteous.

But all these things Elsie kept to herself. On the surface she was a cheerful, friendly, helpful person who would give her right arm to anyone who asked for it.

"In my case, God had to do some plastic surgery on the inside," she would tell some of the girls who had known similar experiences. It began with illnesses. Elsie realized later that many of her illnesses were imagined and that, like her mother, she was trying to call attention to herself. *She* wanted to be the person lying in bed, calling to someone to make her a cup of tea. *She* wanted someone to wait on her, comfort her. If she couldn't get love, she would accept pity.

But eventually, of course, she had love. She had her husband, she had her children, and they loved her very much. She was an affectionate, dedicated wife and mother—and still it was not enough. Having missed love at such an early age, she didn't recognize it when she saw it.

Imagined or not, at the time she had her illnesses, they were very real to her. Sometimes the eczema on her hands and arms was so bad she had to wear cotton gloves day and night. Domestic help was out of the question when she was unable to keep up with the care of her family and her home, but John came up with the perfect solution: Why not ask the welfare department if there was a teen-age girl who would like a home in exchange for some help around the house? Elsie thought it was a wonderful idea. She didn't know then that God wasn't making life easier for her; he was putting her to work.

There were several teen-age girls who came to live in the Benton home, one after another. Each one was troubled, what some people might call "a problem." Yet by the time each one left, she was a whole person. And Elsie Benton herself began to be healed.

She saw that she was not the only person in the world who had missed out on love, and that if she had not known Jesus Christ she probably would have become like one of the girls she wanted so much to help. There was so little between them—or, rather, so much. If she had not been able to turn to Jesus in the times of her unhappiness, the frustration inside her would have turned to something else—perhaps to drink, or even to drugs. That was when she understood that if she really wanted to help these girls, she should try to introduce them to Jesus Christ—not by telling them what he could do for them, but what he had done for her.

Sometimes Elsie found it difficult to avoid preaching. When a girl was hurt, Elsie's immediate reaction was to prescribe something to make the pain go away. But that didn't work. A girl had to find the prescription herself, or its effects didn't last. Elsie had to keep reminding herself that her job was to lead a person to Christ, not to get in his way.

As Elsie began to speak more openly about the protection God had given her, she made a new discovery. God had done far more than protect her from false satisfactions of her human needs; God had loved her from the moment of her creation. Nothing had been hidden from him. He knew all about her resentments, her jealousies, her vanity, and still he loved her deeply. He looked past the role she played and loved the real Elsie, flaws and all. Amazingly, Elsie was coming upon the same truth that was to change the lives of so many young girls. Yes, she knew how they felt, indeed!

If she wanted to know what real love was like, she had only to look to God, where she found no harsh words, no frown of disappointment, no shaking of a head or pointing of a finger. Instead she found comfort for her pain, understanding for her fears, encouragement for the tiniest step in a new direction, help for the times she would fall. And when she looked around her immediate world she found that same love mirrored in a thousand ways—through her husband, her children, the girls who now looked to her as a mother. Mom B—the name was spelled with love. Her life was filled with love!

On the night when she began to realize what was happening to her, Elsie told her husband about it. "John, she said, a bit uncertainly, "I feel as if I've been born all over again."

John pressed her hand and smiled. "Fine thing for a

minister's wife to say," he said, and then both of them cried.

The surgery God had performed on the spiritual being of Elsie Benton may have been invisible, but certain changes began to be apparent—at least to Elsie. The chronic illnesses were gone. The ugly guilt that came from knowing she was not always what she appeared to be was gone. She no longer had to pretend to love everybody. She was free to be a loving person, to give to others what God constantly gave to her.

Elsie was particularly fond of a passage from Job: ". . . he knoweth the way that I take: when he hath tried me, I shall come forth as gold" (23:10). As she watched Sue trying to avoid her that snowy morning, she hoped that someday Sue also would understand what those words meant.

Sue was helping to shovel snow off the path leading to the chapel when she was told that Betty Holiday was waiting to see her. Wherever she went, Betty found her.

"Tell her I'll be there in a few minutes," she called to the girl who had shouted the message from the steps of the house. "I'm almost finished."

One of the other girls would have taken over for her. It wasn't every day that there were visitors. But Sue wanted time to calm down. She was confused by all kinds of feelings—surprise, contempt, anxiety, guilt, and something unnamed she refused to admit.

When she walked into the reception room she was in control, but the moment she saw Betty she felt uneasy. Betty was so willing to be hurt, and Sue wasn't sure she could resist the temptation.

Betty was sitting on the couch in front of the glass wall opposite the entrance. Beyond her Sue could see for miles, now that the trees were bare. The land sloped downward in snow-covered round hills, and at the bottom somewhere was the Hudson River. The sun was shining, and the sky was bright with reflected light. There were very few clouds. Soon the sun would melt the snow.

This time Betty wasn't overcome with pity. Her expression was serious but not grim as she held out her hand. Sue had expected an embrace and steeled herself for it, but it never came. She shook Betty's hand, which was cool and dry. Her own was moist.

"How are you, Sue?" Betty said, looking directly into her eyes. It was not an idle question. She really wanted to know.

Sue looked away. "I don't know how to answer that," she said. "Should I say 'Fine'? 'Better'? Do you want me to say that I'm happy?"

"No, I don't want you to say anything that isn't true—that isn't exactly the way you feel at this moment."

"Okay, then," Sue said, sitting in the chair facing the couch. "Let's say I'm nervous—at this moment I'm nervous."

Betty sat on the couch. She smiled briefly. "At least, that's a good start. Why are you nervous, Sue?"

"Well—you're full of surprises. And I never know how I'm going to react."

"But why do you have to know?"

"Take my word for it," Sue said. "It's better that way."

"No, it isn't," Betty said. "Try something else this time. Try reacting in whatever way you feel to what I have to say. Okay?"

Sue looked down at the floor. She thought it was a mistake to agree, but she nodded. "Okay."

Betty folded her hands tightly in her lap. "Now it's my turn to be nervous," she said, forcing a grin.

She's nice, Sue thought. *She really is a nice person.*

"I want to apologize for the way I behaved the last time I saw you," Betty said.

"Apologize!—*You?*"

Betty held up her hand. "Wait—let me finish, then you'll understand."

Sue sat back in the chair.

"You were a little rough on Frank and me, Sue, but you also were more than a little right. I told Frank what you said—that we didn't want to know the real you. At first he was angry, just as I was. Then, when we began to pray about it, we suddenly understood how you must have felt when you were with us. We *did* want you to be a sweet, uncomplicated girl—partly because we wanted to feel we had something to do with making you that way."

"But you *did* help me," Sue said. She couldn't stand to see Betty taking so much blame upon herself.

"No—God did. Maybe he used us to get through to you. That's all. We can't take credit for that. But we did fail to love you—I mean, really love you the way you were. No matter what you were. You were right. We loved the image you offered, not the girl herself." Betty was trying not to cry and took a deep breath. "I certainly don't want to ruin this visit," she said.

Sue wanted to go to her, to put her arms around her, but she felt awkward. She squirmed in her chair.

"Anyway—I came here to give you another invitation. It's from Frank and me. We think it's wonderful that you're here, and we hope—we pray—that you'll stay until you have everything you need to start your life over." She was more at ease now, and her smile was beautiful. "And when you need a place to live—when you go to school, or whatever you want to do—please come to us. Whatever you are—whoever you are—we love you. You can't make us stop."

Sue looked away from her. She did not want to cry in front of Betty.

Betty stood up and smoothed her skirt. "You don't have to say a word, Sue. We don't want an answer—ever. We just want you to know that we're here." She leaned down and kissed Sue's cheek. Then she was gone.

Sue sat looking out at the snow. The light seemed to be getting brighter, which was strange at that time in the afternoon. Then she realized that the tears in her eyes were intensifying the glitter of the snow. She had never cried like this, never so softly, almost gently. There was no anger in her. The tension she had lived with all her life had relaxed, and she felt as if the soreness was being healed by her tears.

Mom B was standing over her. "Sue—are you all right?"

Even as she was crying, Sue smiled. It was a large smile that completely reshaped her face and made it lovely. "I'm all right, Mom B," she said, nodding. She had never called Elsie by that name before. "I've been forgiven."

"I can see," Elsie said. "You're beautiful!"

Like a small child, Sue reached out toward Elsie. "It's so good to be loved," she said. "I've just got to hug somebody. Mom B—let me hug you, please!"

CHAPTER 11

John Benton had a small office on the top floor of the house. He liked to work there at night. During the day there were too many other things to do, things that seemed to make more sense than paperwork.

On a warm night in July 1975, John Benton climbed the stairs slowly, feeling more tired with each step. It wasn't the heat or the number of stairs that was getting him. It was the report on his desk. He had already gone through it once, quickly. Tonight he had to read it carefully.

The report informed him that some of the Teen Challenge centers for girls were going to close down. A shortage of money or too many troubled girls—either way you looked at it, the result was unbelievable. Would Teen Challenge really have to turn away some girls? Dave Wilkerson didn't think so. He wanted the surviving centers to take in the girls from the ones that closed. What about The Walter Hoving Home? How many girls could it accommodate?

There was room for a few more. If necessary, they could squeeze in more than a few. But The Walter Hoving Home was having similar problems—there wasn't enough money to support all the girls the Home took in.

Food, utilities, books and lesson materials, equipment, and repairs ate away at the annual contributions. Prices of everything kept going up, and in hard times people cut down on their donations.

Benton had already put the girls on an economy program—no unnecessary phone calls; turn off the lights when you leave a room; don't use a car if you can walk or ride a bicycle; eat your food, don't waste it; use both sides of a sheet of paper. Everything helped. But not enough. Much as he dreaded facing it, the old obstacle was there again—more money. Each time their need had been answered miraculously, Benton thought the problem had been solved for good. He should have known better.

The foundation wouldn't be able to help this time. They had bent their regulations as far as they could. Who else was there? Benton had sent out an appeal through the Home's mailing list, and that helped, but, again, not enough. He could think of a number of individuals who had given generously and repeatedly in the past. Could he ask them for still more?

It wasn't a question of *could,* he decided. Sometimes there were things a person had to do. He really didn't know any other way.

He sat down at his desk and picked up the report that lay on top of a pile of papers. He could hear the steady whirring of the crickets down below, and the sweet-scented night breeze was just beginning to come through the screened windows.

No matter how carefully he read the report, he couldn't find a word of hope in it. But there was Dave, moving ahead and knocking on doors he was confident would open. Benton couldn't say "No," he knew that. When Wilkerson asked him how many girls the Home could accept, he would have to reply with a number, not an excuse.

Benton looked at his watch. It was getting too late. First thing in the morning he would call Walter Hoving.

CHAPTER 12

It was Walter Hoving's custom to walk through Tiffany & Co. as often as he could get away from his desk. He did it without fanfare. He enjoyed being close to the people who came into his store—some to browse, some to purchase, some to set foot inside the door just to say they had been there. The first-floor salespeople noticed more and more tourists stopping in; Tiffany's was becoming a landmark. That was fine with Hoving. He thought it was encouraging when people went out of their way to see something beautiful—and everything in Tiffany's was beautiful. He was proud of that tradition.

Beauty was important to Hoving. Its presence in the world was a reminder of God's genius. Only God could create beauty with ease; human beings had to work at it. But God had given man the tools with which to create the beautiful: an ability to see something that did not yet exist, a body whose parts could be trained to perform incredibly intricate motions, and patience to stay with an idea through many failures. Beauty, to Hoving, also was man's way of thanking God for his generosity.

Hoving was alarmed at the increasing amount of ugliness in the world. He wondered why so many people put up with it when they could have taken a stand against it.

He smiled at the memory of times when he had taken such stands. Yes, he had spoken up for his beliefs, but he had had fun doing it, and he thought it was a good idea to have a little fun in business. Years ago he had fought an attempt to build a restaurant on the edge of Central Park, one of the loveliest wooded areas in the world. He had won that battle. And once he took on the First National City Bank for erecting a huge, metal, brightly lighted Christmas tree on Park Avenue. In his opinion, it was one of the ugliest things he had ever seen. To make his point he wrote the copy for an ad that appeared in *The Wall Street Journal* and began: "Dear First National City Bank: We are very sad to see that you are once again polluting the aesthetic atmosphere of Park Avenue by lighting that loud and vulgar Christmas tree." The tree was erected for one more year and then it disappeared, so Hoving decided he had won that battle, too.

He had lost the battle to keep Fifth Avenue traffic running both ways. It went only downtown now, a change that Hoving believed had begun the erosion of Fifth Avenue's character—slowly at first, but more rapidly in recent years. Some of the great old stores had moved or gone out of business. Too many businesses that had nothing to do with fashion were moving in, which meant that there were fewer and fewer windows offering marvelous things to see.

He turned away from his desk and looked out one of the enormous windows behind him. The intersection of Fifth Avenue and 57th Street always was stimulating—when people all over the world mentioned "Fifth Avenue," this was what they meant. It was more than one of the most exciting retail areas in the world; it was the creative heart of the fashion marketplace. You could see it in the department store windows, you could hear it in the impatient sounding of car horns and the brakes of buses; you felt it as you walked at a fast pace to keep up with men and women who had somewhere to go—something new was happening, an idea was taking shape, somebody was introducing a design that would change the way people lived. But on this day Walter Hoving didn't see any of it.

Ever since John Benton had called him earlier that morning, there was only one thing on his mind, and that was the Home—and how to get enough money to keep it open. A while ago Benton had taken out a twenty-five-thousand-dollar bank loan to pay some of the operating expenses. He thought he would be able to pay it back quickly as more contributions came in, but he hadn't figured on a recession in the economy. Nobody had. Now the bankers wanted their money. If they called in the note, that would be the end. And even if the Home could get the twenty-five-thousand-dollars, how would they pay the next month's bills? Somehow they had to pull ahead. There were so many big projects that needed attention. The driveway ought to be paved. The dining room had to be enlarged. If the Home took in girls under seventeen, they had to be given the equivalent of a high-school education. That meant more staff, more equipment, and classrooms and books.

Hoving got up and walked to the door of his office. The door was open, as usual. He liked to be available to anyone who wanted to come in and talk. All his employees knew they were welcome anytime, especially if they had a problem. If someone was sick, or depressed, or in trouble of any kind, he could talk to Walter Hoving. He could pray with Walter Hoving, too. And if he didn't want to pray, he knew he would be in Hoving's prayers. It was a good feeling and one of the reasons why so many

Tiffany employees considered themselves members of a family.

He changed his mind and went back to his desk to call his wife. Pauline would want to know about the Home. She had been in on it from the beginning.

When a newspaper reporter once asked Walter Hoving if he considered himself a religious man, the answer was, "Only for the last forty years. That's when I married my wife. She reformed me."

It was true. God had reached out to him through Pauline. She was a day-by-day example of Christian love. In fact, it was Pauline who had brought him into contact with Teen Challenge. He couldn't remember exactly how many years ago she had called him at his office to tell him about David Wilkerson, a young country preacher she had invited to lunch later in the week. Wilkerson, she said, wanted to work in the city streets, trying to reach warring gang members and bring them the message that only God could help them stop destroying themselves and each other. Wilkerson had already made converts out of some of the most hardened gang members. Now he needed a place where his converts could come to get in out of the street, where they could see that there were others like them, others who wanted to learn how to live the kind of life God meant them to have. In other words, Wilkerson needed help, and money was not enough. He needed to meet the kind of people who could understand what he was trying to do and could talk about it to others. Pauline wanted to invite a few of those people to lunch with Wilkerson.

"Fine," Hoving had said. He agreed with his wife that the group should be kept small so that everyone could get to know Wilkerson. Then he suggested a few names. Pauline added a few more. By the next day the "small group" had turned into thirty-two people, far too many for the Hoving dining room. They would have to meet at the River Club restaurant on the first floor of the Hovings' apartment building.

Since that day Teen Challenge had become an important part of the Hovings' life. They had seen it grow from a single house on a Brooklyn street into a nationwide organization. It reached beyond the cities and into the suburbs to touch the souls of thousands of young people. Today there weren't so many gang members or even drug addicts. Times had changed and so had the problems of the people caught in its shifting sands. Teen Challenge found itself ministering to fear, rejection, hopelessness, to the inability to love and the loss of identity. These illnesses expressed themselves as vandalism, shoplifting, mugging, prostitution, alcoholism, running away from home, burglary. But the real source of all the trouble was that people were going their own way rather than God's.

There had been a lot of crises in Teen Challenge's past, and Hoving had seen many solutions come from nowhere. John Benton was right to call them "miracles."

Well, that was what the Home needed right now. Another miracle. A big one.

They had time, perhaps another few months. Hoving had known amazing things to happen within days, hours, even minutes. Over the years he had become a patient man who knew that God worked with the very raw materials of human life—a mind, the senses, green grass, trees and flowers, city streets and sidewalks, animals, birds, and even bank accounts. And why not? God had been here. He knew how we were.

Yes, there was time. The Home could wait for God to make his move.

CHAPTER 13

On Thursday of that week Hoving left his office at five-fifteen and walked the few blocks to St. Bartholomew's Episcopal Church. No matter how many times he saw the enormous cluster of buildings at the corner of Park Avenue and East 50th Street, he was excited by it. This was a city church, landscaped in concrete. Its mission was somewhat different from churches in less crowded parts of the world because its congregation needed more than spiritual nourishment. Many of them lived in a single room or a small apartment. Many were far from home and relatives and friends. They needed such basic things as exercise, a well-balanced meal, someone to talk to, or someone to listen. In a way, St Bart's had become like one of the early Christian churches—a twenty-four-hour-a-day community, although, of course, its facilities were up to date. They included a gymnasium, a pool, a library, an auditorium, meeting rooms, and a lounge called The Grille, where young people could get a snack or a complete meal at a low price.

Every Thursday evening at five-thirty a group of men and women met in the basement-level library where, at certain times of the year, the low angle of the sun slanted rays through the windows where they shone like sheer ribbons of gold against the dark wood of the bookshelves lining the room from floor to ceiling. The group had been meeting there for several years, ever since Walter Hoving stood up during an after-services reception and announced that he would be in the library on Thursday evening. He wanted to talk about Jesus Christ and what he meant in a person's life. It would be wonderful, he said, to meet with others who wanted to do the same.

About five people showed up at the first meeting. In later weeks the group increased and then decreased again. It never was the same size. Some people heard about the meetings and came as they were passing through the city. Others came for short periods of time as they were going through a crisis. Some came regularly because they could not live as fully without it.

The group called itself by no particular name. It was simply the Thursday evening witness group. They spoke freely, or spoke not at all if they chose. But the theme was always the same: How is Jesus Christ affecting the way I live?

Eleanor McManus was already in the library when Hoving arrived. She always arrived first, which was not a simple accomplishment, because, according to her doctors, Eleanor McManus was not supposed to be able to go anywhere at all on her own.

Mrs. McManus used to manage The Grille at St. Bartholomew's. Short, auburn-haired, motherly-featured, she was a favorite with the young men and women—many of them new to the city—who used to come to The Grille. She knew them all and loved them all and shared with them the pains of growing up.

Two years ago, just before Christmastime, Eleanor McManus had a stroke. Her left side was totally paralyzed, but, they told her, she was lucky to be alive. She would regain some movement, but not enough to get around by herself. At best, she would be confined to a wheelchair. There were worse things than that, they said.

They didn't really understand. Eleanor McManus was alone in the world. She loved and needed her daily contact with people. There could hardly be anything worse than confining her to a wheelchair for the rest of her life.

"I'm no theologian," she told the witness group one night, "but I've always loved God, and I knew he loved me. Jesus is right here with us, that's how I know. So, one day, after they sent me home from the hospital, I decided to ask God to help me. After all, the doctors had tried everything they could, and I had tried everything *I* could—so I felt it was time to try God."

Not for one moment did she doubt that God was going to heal her; still, she wanted to be sure that he got the credit for it. She would take none for herself or for anyone else.

She was alone in her apartment. She wheeled her chair to the front door and with her right hand reached up and slid the chain across the door. She turned the lock and wheeled herself back across the room.

"Dear Lord," she prayed, "I've locked myself in, and I'm not going to get out until I can walk. That door is going to stay locked, and nobody is going to get in until I can walk across the room on both my legs and open that door with my left hand. Now, you know *I* can't do it, Lord, but *you* can. You can make me walk."

She was perspiring as she got ready to lift herself from the chair. She knew her right hand would grasp the chair arm. Her left arm, until that moment, had been numb, motionless. But, as she told the group, she did not have to struggle at all. "God lifted me up and let me walk across that room just the way I had always done it. And when I got to the door I raised my left hand and took the chain off the door and turned the lock. Then I walked back to my wheelchair just as steady as you please." She eventually became 90 per cent ambulatory. "God did that," she always told them.

Mrs. McManus was especially pleased that Walter Hoving had also arrived a few minutes early, because she wanted to talk to him before the meeting began. She was troubled, she said, by the many people, especially young ones, who came to her with their problems. "You know, even though I'm retired from The Grille, they still remember me and come to see me. And I wish I could do more for them, but I'm not an educated person, and I just don't know what to tell them to do. So I tell them the only thing *I* know how to do—try God."

Hoving smiled. "I wish more 'educated' people knew as much as you do, Mrs. McManus," he said.

She would accept no compliment and waved it away. "I'm getting older, and I get tired, and I can't talk to everybody who comes to see me. So, since I know what I'm going to tell them anyway, I was wondering if I could wear some sort of a pin—made with the words 'try God.' What do you think of that, Mr. Hoving?"

It wasn't a bad idea at all, Hoving decided. Some people might not be comfortable with such an easygoing relationship with God, but many others were seeking it. That was what the witness group was all about. That was why so many people came to church—it was the house of God, and they wanted to inhabit it. They wanted to try God.

"I like the idea," he said.

"Then could you make me a pin like that?" she said. "I don't know where else I can get one made."

Tiffany's had had more unusual requests, Hoving had to admit. The only difficulty would be making one pin for one customer. It would be expensive.

Other members of the witness group were arriving. "Let me think about it, all right?" Hoving said.

That was fine with Mrs. McManus. "Maybe you'll have something by next Thursday?" she said.

Hoving nodded and did not dare let her see the smile that crossed his mind. There would be no putting off Mrs. McManus.

The walk back to his apartment after the meeting was always pleasant on a summer evening. New York was peaceful, almost lazy at that time of day. There were fewer people on the streets, and they walked more slowly, stopping to look in shop windows for as long as they pleased. You could get a taxi.

Walter Hoving was thinking about Mrs. McManus's pin. One was out of the question. He would have to find more people who wanted to wear such a pin so that the unit cost could be brought within reach. In fact, a pin like that should be very inexpensive so that everybody could have one. *Everybody ought to try God.*

It didn't seem right for Tiffany's to make a profit on the pin. Costs had to be covered, naturally, but if there were any profits to be made, they should go to a worthy cause. Charities, religious charities especially, might be able to use a pin for fund-raising. And what about the members of St. Bart's itself? It was a large congregation, and the church always needed money.

But that wasn't everybody—and everybody ought to try

God. If everybody bought that pin, there would be enough money for St. Bart's, for The Walter Hoving Home, and for who knows what else!

Hoving began to walk faster as the idea took shape. God may have been using Mrs. McManus to save the Home—Hoving wasn't going to question it. He had other things to do, such as finding a way to produce the pin and finding a way to tell everybody about it.

CHAPTER 14

Anne Balsan had been Walter Hoving's secretary for two years. She was accustomed to the unusual.

This morning Hoving had spent most of his time at his desk—doodling, from what Anne could see from her desk outside his office. He would sketch something on a piece of paper and sit back to look at it. He was deep in concentration. Whatever it was, Anne knew it would be interesting.

"Anne, will you come in here for a moment—I want to show you something," he said from the doorway.

He showed her the piece of paper. He had drawn the words "Try God" in every imaginable way—one word over the other, one word alongside the other, one word indented under the other, in curving lines, a circle, a right angle. He used all kinds of letters, from simple to ornate.

"Which one do you like best?" he asked.

She looked at each one and allowed her feelings to make the decision. It didn't take long. "That one," she said, pointing to the sketch of one word over the other in clear Tiffany Classic letters.

"Why that one?" he asked, as she knew he would. Good design was not achieved by accident. Beauty had a message, and he would want to know whether the message was understood.

"Because it's beautiful," she said, "and because it says everything it has to say simply and honestly."

"I agree," he said, and reached for the phone. His sketch was only a suggestion. John Brown, head of the design department, would perfect it.

A week later, on Thursday morning, the Home's Advisory Board held its quarterly meeting in one of Tiffany's conference rooms.

The Board had existed since 1971 and was composed of Christians whose experience in business and the professions enabled them to advise the Home how to raise enough money to keep its doors open. It was different from the Board of Directors in that these people only made suggestions, which no one was obliged to take. Their most important contribution was their dedication and enthusiasm in spreading the word that there was such a place as The Walter Hoving Home. They gave generously from their own pockets and persuaded many of their business associates to do the same. At Christmastime they invited the girls' choir to sing in their offices; they invited some of the girls to their churches to tell their fellow parishioners how Jesus Christ had changed their lives; if the Home planned a fund-raising event, they not only got some of the best speakers, but also sold enough tickets to leave some guests standing. For all their hard work, the Home was still in trouble, which is why the meeting was so somber.

The committee reports were grim. They finished whatever hopes the members might have had for an answer to their most recent prayers. Only Hoving seemed untouched by the bad news. Near the end of the meeting he passed around a sheet of paper and asked everyone to take a good look at it. It was the design for a pin, he said, and he wanted to know what they thought of it.

Without exception, everyone liked the design, but no one was excited about it. Why was he showing it to them at a time like this?

"Because," Hoving said, retrieving the paper and holding up in front of him, "Tiffany is going to make this pin and sell it. And the proceeds will go to the Home."

That was different. That was wonderful! The atmosphere of the meeting changed immediately.

"But won't you have to sell it by the thousands?" someone asked.

"We will," Hoving said.

"Can you do that? I mean, will enough people buy it?"

"They will."

"Walter, how are you going to tell people about it?"

Hoving had that look in his eye that said he was going to take a stand and have a little fun doing it. "We're going to run an ad in *The New York Times,*" he said.

Later, though, he had to admit that no one else was as confident as he was.

CHAPTER 15

Sue had been at the Home for almost seven months. In another month she would get a pass to go home for a week. She dreaded it.

She really didn't know where "home" was. She had an aunt who lived in the town where she was born and barely remembered her. She had no desire to see her foster parents, if they were still alive. Frank and Betty Holiday—well, they were friends, not family.

The staff at the home urged—insisted, really—that the girls go home. They allowed them four days to visit, plus two days for travel. Most of the girls felt as Sue did: They were afraid. Their lives were so different now, and they didn't want to face old temptations. They had too much to lose. But, for the same reasons, the staff felt it was necessary for the girls to see their families and friends, to walk once more in the environment they had barely survived. The girls were stronger than they realized, and the staff knew of no better way for them to find that out.

Sue had already gone out on two short "passes," as they were called. When a girl had been at the Home for four months she was allowed to go out for a day in the company of a few other girls and a favorite counselor. Usually they took a train into New York City and spent the day there doing whatever they pleased—roller skating, attending the opera or the theater, having dinner in a restaurant. They had to be back in the Home that night. After six months a girl got another pass of the same kind.

At seven months a girl could spend a day by herself in the city, but usually she took a friend with her. In Sue's case, it was Betty Holiday.

Sue thought Mom B must have known she was nervous because she asked Sue to join her and a group of girls who were going to speak at a church in Garrison. "Speak" was the word Mom B used for "testify," and when you testified you told people what your life used to be and what it was now. Sue had seen many of the girls do it, and she had been helped by their stories, so she didn't mind being asked. She wanted to tell people what Christ had done for her. She just wished she had a better story to tell. She was an ex-convict—the Home deserved a better representative.

"Don't spend so much time thinking about your past," her counselor said when Sue told her how she felt. "Think about the way you are now."

What a difference! Sue thought. She had regained the weight she had lost those last few months in jail. Her eyes were clear and her expression gentle. Her hair, always frizzy when it was long, was short and curly. She wore contact lenses instead of the metal-rimmed glasses. But she rarely wore anything fancier than blue jeans and a simple blouse. There were prettier clothes in her closet, and someday she would wear them to a special event—perhaps to the church that evening—but she knew now she did not need them to look her best.

Sue liked the routine of the Home. She always had. But then, she had always been an early riser. Some of the girls had trouble getting up at 7 A.M. Some weren't accustomed to eating breakfast. Almost all of them found prayer a new experience, and at first they thought the staff was joking when they were assigned to classes in Bible study. Even Sue, who had enjoyed school, didn't look forward to memorizing Scripture passages.

The classes weren't at all what she or the other girls had expected. They were conversations between the girls and teachers who cared very deeply what became of them. In this atmosphere the Bible was no longer an intellectual exercise; it became the key to life itself. If a girl had a problem, she could find its solution in God's own words. After forcing herself to attend a few classes, Sue couldn't wait to go to the next one.

And that wasn't all. The girls were taught how to sit and stand and walk gracefully. They learned how to dress and arrange their hair and apply makeup. A course in public speaking gave them the confidence to put their thoughts and feelings into words.

Sue's favorite class was held every other Saturday morning. It was Brother Benton's course in Successful Motivation—which, he said, was something he needed as much as they did. To give them an example he told them about the morning he was driving into the city—"And I love to get on a wide-open road and just go!" he confessed. But that day he found himself behind a state trooper and had to maintain the legal speed limit for most of the trip.

"Finally I couldn't stand it any longer, and I pulled out. As I passed him—I wasn't going more than ten miles above the speed limit—he switched on his loudspeaker and bellowed, 'The legal speed for this road is fifty-five miles per hour!'"

Brother Benton shook his head. "I hated that guy—and I won't repeat what I said to him under my breath. But I slowed down. Then the trooper took the next exit, and just to get even with him I went twice as fast as I ever did."

The girls laughed. They could identify with him.

Benton spread his arms wide. "But you see, I was motivated by my resentment—and I could have killed myself. Maybe somebody else, too."

Debbie raised her hand. "Okay, Brother B, but what *can* you do in a situation like that?"

Benton dropped his arms and smiled. "I Corinthians 13," he said. Debbie frowned.

"You think that's just a bunch of numbers, don't you? Well, you're right—except that they may be the most important numbers in your life." He turned around and picked up a Bible from his desk. Then he read to them:

"'Love is very patient and kind, never jealous or envious, never boastful or proud, never haughty or selfish or rude. Love does not demand its own way. It is not irritable or touchy. It does not hold grudges and will hardly even notice when others do it wrong. It is never glad about injustice, but rejoices whenever truth wins out. If you love someone you will be loyal to him no matter what the cost. You will always believe in him, always expect the best of him, and always stand your ground in defending him.'"

He put the Bible back on the desk. "If you want to know what to do in just about any situation in your life, then you'll find the answer here in these words. But the words aren't enough. Memorizing them isn't enough. We have to act them out. That morning on the road I was impatient—because I failed to *act out* patience. I failed to *act out* kindness toward that trooper. And I sure succeeded in being irritable and touchy."

That's the way Brother B was—and the girls loved him

for it. He never criticized them or anything they did. He aways used his own mistakes as examples, never theirs. Nor did he pretend that it was easy for a person to learn new habits.

"You have to be careful how you respond emotionally to the things that happen in life," he told them. "Once, when one of our neighbors was making my life miserable, I asked God to burn his house down." The girls shrieked with pleasure.

"That's the truth," he said. "Fortunately God knows enough to ignore that kind of prayer. But I'm just trying to show you how much damage we can do when we allow the wrong things to motivate us."

After class that day Sue and several of the girls walked up the hill toward the house, singing a catchy tune composed by an earlier graduate who must have felt the same way they did:

We love you, Brother B,
Oh yes, we do,
We love you, Brother B,
And we'll be true—
We love you, Brother B, we do,
O Brother B, we love you!

It was raining and they lifted their faces toward the gray sky, enjoying the cool drops that fell on them. Their arms were linked, and they kept in step. Suddenly Sue realized that she was as happy as she could possibly be. She could not imagine anything more wonderful in life than the closeness, the friendship, and the understanding of these girls. They loved her. They had helped her forget what it was to be lonely and unwanted. The Bentons loved her, and so did everyone on the staff. They had found an even deeper level of her being, one that lay far beneath the rage she had mistaken for her real self. They had found her kind, helpful, hungry to give love, and she was beginning to accept this evaluation of herself.

She knew then what she was going to say at the church meeting that evening. Each girl was asked to speak for three minutes, but Sue didn't think she would need that much time. "I'm not an ex-convict," she was going to tell them. "I'm not an ex-anything. I am a child of God."

CHAPTER 16

"You people just ruined my property! I'm going to sue you!" It was John Benton's favorite neighbor, a man who continued to find fault with the simple fact that the Home existed.

"What happened?" Benton asked.

"My land is covered with mud, that's what happened! You went and drained your pool, didn't you!"

"It isn't the pool," Benton tried to explain. "It's been raining for three days, and that mud is coming from higher up the mountain."

"But you did drain your pool, didn't you?"

"No. We can't. It's full of mud."

"Well, so is my property! What are you going to do about it?"

One thing the Home did not need was a lawsuit. But Benton did not have an answer.

A heavy rain had fallen for three days, washing dirt and stones and leaves and roots down from the mountain above the Home. When the skies cleared, the pool was almost filled with mud. It couldn't be drained, but that didn't make any difference to their neighbor.

"He seems to think we invented rain," Benton said to his wife.

He didn't want to admit it, but he knew his neighbor had a leg to stand on. At the end of each summer they did drain the water out of the pool by opening the dam, and the water gushed down onto the neighbor's property. With it went much of the silt that had accumulated on the pool bottom. Benton didn't know of any other way to get rid of it.

"It washed away some of his grass," Elsie said. "You can't blame him for getting mad."

"Whose side are you on?"

When he looked into the cost of having the mud removed from the pool, Benton smacked his hand against his forehead. "Six thousand dollars!" Elsie winced.

"The money isn't there, that's all there is to it," Benton said.

"Maybe the girls could help us dig it out," Elsie suggested.

"Honey, it would take a bulldozer—or a tractor. Not a shovel. Not even fifty shovels." Then he realized what he had said. "Of course—a tractor! Maybe we can rent one."

John Benton had never operated a tractor. Neither had anyone else on the staff. Well, he would learn. For one thousand dollars he was able to rent a heavy tractor and a pickup truck. He was clumsy at first, but within a few hours he learned how to push the thick mud in the direction of the truck. Truckload after truckload went down the driveway, some to neighbors who wanted it for fill, some to a dumping ground.

Benton's favorite neighbor had refused the mud. "I don't want the dirty old stuff," he growled. "I need some clean, decent dirt."

Benton shrugged. Perhaps there was no pleasing this man; still, he had to try. The man was difficult, but he may have had his reasons. He was ill and he lived alone. Perhaps he was afraid and didn't know any other way to express it.

On one of his trips along the road to the dumping ground, Benton had noticed an excavation. Someone was digging a foundation, and alongside the hole was a large hill of dirt—"clean, decent dirt." He wondered if anyone was going to use it. No harm in asking. He got in the truck and drove to the site. It was four-thirty, almost quitting time for the men on the bulldozers. Benton located the foreman, and when he asked him what he was going to do with all that dirt, the foreman said, "Get rid of it, I guess. Would you like some?"

"Would I!"

"Help yourself."

The foreman helped Benton load the dirt into his pickup truck. "Never saw anybody get so excited over a pile of dirt," he laughed.

The truck was so heavy that Benton had to drive slowly, taking the country-road curves with care. He drove past the Home and down the road until he came to his favorite neighbor's driveway. Parking the truck at the entrance, he walked up the hill to the house.

After he rang the bell he waited for a long time, or so it seemed. He was disappointed. Perhaps no one was home. Then the door opened.

Benton didn't give him a chance to complain. "Would you like some clean, decent dirt?" he said, grinning. Seeing the angry look on his neighbor's face he added, "Seriously. I have a load of the most beautiful dirt in the world—in my truck, right over there."

From the doorway the neighbor could see the truck. He squinted at it, considered Benton with suspicion, and went down the driveway to examine the offer. "You didn't have to do this," he grumbled when he saw the dirt. "I didn't mean for you to go to all this trouble."

"No trouble," Benton said.

"Must have cost you something, though."

"It's free. Believe me." Benton held out his hand. "We're your neighbors, you know. And neighbors ought to help each other."

"That pool's a big problem for me," he complained.

"You're right," Benton said. "But we learned something from all this rain. Now we know how to clean the pool without ruining your grass."

The man's hand shook a little as he accepted Benton's. He didn't exactly smile, but he wasn't scowling anymore, either. "You're a nice guy, Mr. Benton," he said. "A nice guy."

On the way back, Benton realized that the rain had created an opportunity which the Home should not pass up. There probably were many ways in which they could help their neighbors. That was going to be his next project once the Home got out of its financial troubles.

If the Home got out, he reminded himself.

CHAPTER 17

To Anne Balsan, Walter Hoving was a "loving perfectionist." He didn't mind how hard he had to work on an idea to get it right; yet he never became irritable, even when he had to start all over from scratch.

Every now and then Anne looked toward Hoving's office, where she could see him working on a new Tiffany ad. He often wrote the copy himself because he knew exactly what he wanted to say, and writing it out was easier than telling someone else. But this ad must have been special, because he obviously was having a hard time satisfying himself. Again and again he would cross out a phrase, a word, sometimes the entire ad. Finally he sat back and read what he had written, and from the expression on his face Anne knew the ad was ready to be set in type. Hoving nodded to himself, got up, and brought the copy out to her desk. He didn't wait for her to read it.

Under a black-and-white photograph of the pin, the ad read:

"This is a limited edition; that is, limited to people who believe in God. A pendant for women and a pin for both men and women of Tiffany sterling silver or Vermeil. The entire proceeds will be donated by Tiffany to The Walter Hoving Home, Inc., in Garrison, New York—a nonsectarian center for drug-addicted and seriously troubled girls—where, after a year's treatment, over 90 per cent are permanently cured by accepting God into their lives. In sterling silver, $10. Vermeil, $12."

Beneath that were the familiar Tiffany & Co. trademark, a special number for telephone orders, and Tiffany's address.

Anne felt a little misty-eyed. It was a beautiful ad, as beautiful and honest as the pin itself. But what a risk Hoving would take by printing it. A business usually didn't take a public stand for God, and there were some in Tiffany who argued against it. Hoving was responsible to a Board of Directors who would be very disturbed by a wave of public indignation. And of all places for the ad to appear for the first time—in New York City.

On Friday, September 12, 1975, the ad appeared on page 3 in *The New York Times.*

Later some people would say that on Saturday morning people were lined up outside Tiffany waiting for the store to open so they could buy a pin or a pendant. But that wasn't the way it really happened.

Some of the salesclerks on the first floor hadn't read the ad and were a bit puzzled when someone asked, "Where can I get the 'Try God' pin?" It happened a number of times. Inquiries were directed to the silver department on the second floor.

Mrs. Elizabeth Willard, a member of the management of the silver department, noticed that there were a few more customers than usual on the second floor. She was glad to see that the new pin was selling—it was good for people to know they could buy something in Tiffany's for such a modest price.

Up on the fifth floor, in the mail order department, the

staff was getting panicky. There weren't enough lines to handle the incoming calls from people who wanted "the 'Try God' pin." Mrs. Shirley Krug, head of the mail order department, took a lot of the calls herself. She would have to get more help for the rest of the week. Rushed as she was, she had to admit it was pleasant work. Most of the callers were friendly and conversational. They said they were startled—and grateful—to see the word "God" in an ad. Many of them said they had a daughter or a niece or a friend who was in trouble, and they were comforted to know that there was a home where girls could go for help. "A lot of customers are ordering more than one pin or pendant," Mrs. Krug told Walter Hoving. "I think they like the idea of helping the Home."

Later that day Hoving took a call from NBC-TV reporter Carl Stokes. What was happening at Tiffany's? What about this pin he saw advertised in the paper? NBC would like to look into the story and possibly get it on film for one of their news programs. Okay?

Okay. Very okay. "You go up to Garrison and see the Home. Talk to the girls," Hoving said. "There's your story."

Stokes said he would do that, and Hoving gave him John Benton's telephone number.

More calls were waiting for him, but Hoving took a few moments out. He wanted to thank his Lord. As he had told a newspaper reporter who wanted to know who got the idea for the pin, "It was God's idea." He knew, too, that God had found a way to tell everybody about the pin: publicity.

Instead of falling off during the week, the orders increased. Now the telephone calls were coming from the suburbs, and orders were coming by mail from all parts of the country. Mrs. Krug decided that, yes, she would get more help. On the second floor, Mrs. Willard noticed that sales of the pin were holding steady; that was unusual.

By the end of the week one thousand pins and pendants had been sold.

Someone said, "Let's run the ad again." But Hoving said, "Wait. We can do that later. We're getting enough publicity—and it's free."

He was right. NBC-TV had run a sixteen-minute documentary of the Home on the six o'clock news. Several newspaper editorials mentioned the pin, and some even reprinted the ad itself as part of the story. "We couldn't *buy* this kind of publicity," Hoving thought.

One day when Hoving was attending a Christian fund-raising event, Billy Graham got into the elevator with him. The two had been friends for years. When Graham saw the pin in Hoving's lapel, he asked where he could get one.

"You can get it here," Hoving said. Smiling, he removed his pin and gave it to Graham. "I've got more."

"Good," Graham said, "because I'd like to order a lot more." He wanted to offer it, free, to his television viewers on New Year's Eve. Hoving said that Tiffany might be able to donate some. Graham's television crusades reached an enormous number of people. "Wouldn't it be great if more people really did try God," Hoving said.

Anne Balsan had begun keeping a file of letters that accompanied some of the orders. They were special. One of them came from a prisoner in the Virginia Correctional Center for Women:

"I hope I'm not too late with my order for three (3) pins, TRY GOD. . . . I had to wait until the money I earned this month was put on the books before I could write a disbursement slip.

"With *maximum* pay being $13 *per month* for a 5 day week at 8 hours a day, you can understand the reason for my delay . . .

"I'm looking forward to receiving them and I know the persons wearing them will be ecstatic, as they have dedicated their lives to His service.

"God bless you all for the great comfort that The Walter Hoving Home brings to so many people."

From Pueblo, Colorado, a mother of four girls wrote: "My husband, who is a brand-new Christian, wants a TRY GOD pin to wear, so he can have an opportunity to witness more about Jesus."

The Jewish Theological Seminary of America sent a copy of a clipping from its newspaper, *The Jewish Post:* "At the Jewish Theological Seminary, Rabbi Seymour Siegel is sporting a sterling silver lapel pin proclaiming: TRY GOD. It was sent to him as a gift by a former pupil who purchased it at the elite Tiffany's of Fifth Avenue. All proceeds of the sales go to drug addict rehabilitation via religion, a slip in the Tiffany box notes."

The "slip" in the box was actually the inside of the box cover, on which the original ad was reprinted. That had been Anne Balsan's suggestion. It was a little reminder that there was such a place as The Walter Hoving Home, and that its girls needed help.

On Friday, late in the afternoon, a tall, powerful-looking man asked the guard on the first floor of Tiffany's, "Is this where I can get that 'Try God' pin?" His face was flushed, and he was hot. He was a jewelry buyer, but his quest today had nothing to do with business. He had been all over the city trying to get one of those pins he had seen advertised in the *Times*, but wherever he went he was told, "Only Tiffany has them." He wanted a pin for his niece, who had a way of finding trouble. Liz had smashed up three cars, and at nineteen she was almost an alcoholic. She should have been arrested on more than one charge, but either she or her parents always talked the police out of it.

Liz's uncle was not a religious man, but when he saw the Tiffany ad in the *Times*, he felt as if it had been written especially for Liz. She needed help, but not the kind she could get in an institution. She had been in several of those—sometimes committed by her father when he could think of nothing else to do about her, and sometimes by herself in sheer disgust for the things she did and could not remember. All she ever got were pills, as if she needed them with all the pot and liquor she consumed. Her cure, if you could call it that, lasted as long as it took her to get from the hospital to the nearest bottle on the day of her discharge.

But this Walter Hoving Home, with its 90 per cent rate of cure, was different. Nothing else had worked for Liz, so why not try God?

CHAPTER 18

"Hey, how pretty!" She took the pendant out of the box and brought it to him. "Thanks, Uncle Lou. Will you put it on for me?" She turned around and pushed up her thick blond hair so he could fasten the clasp around her neck.

Lou was relieved. She liked it.

Liz ran into her room to look in the mirror. She came back quickly and hugged her uncle. "I'll treasure it—forever!" She was winding him around her little finger, and he knew it. She always did that. As soon as he left, she would probably put the pendant in her drawer and forget about it.

"Did you read it?" he asked her.

"Sure," she said. " 'Try God.' " She tilted her head and smiled at him impishly. "Do you really think I should?"

"Yes, I do—and I mean it." He picked up the box cover and gave it to her. "Here's something else I mean. Read it, and think about it."

She twisted her round face into a comic frown and read the copy aloud, mocking it with a deep voice and dramatic flourishes. When she finished, she waited for Lou to laugh. He didn't.

"Does this have something to do with *me?*" she said. "This Home up in who-knows-where?" Then she stared at him for a moment. "You think I ought to go there?" she said in the helpless, childlike tone he knew too well. It meant she wanted him to say "No." She wanted him to tell her she wasn't that bad, that there was nothing really wrong with her that time wouldn't cure. She was high-strung, nervous, whatever. Lou had already been through every excuse, and still it was hard to resist giving in to her when she sat all huddled up on a kitchen stool.

"You're a good kid," he began and caught himself—"Yes, I think you should go there."

Again her mood changed, and she stood up as if she had to get somewhere in a hurry. Uncle Lou was dismissed from her attention. "Okay," she said casually as she left, "Maybe I will."

As soon as her uncle was gone, Liz came out of her room and went down to the basement. She opened a cardboard box and dug down into a pile of old clothes until she found a bottle of liquor she had hidden there. She had put it there a long time ago—long for her, anyway. She had not had a drink in ten days. Nor had she taken pills or pot, either. Now she had a special reason to break her fast: She wanted to stop thinking—about anything.

No one else was in the house, and she would be alone for hours. Her mother was probably off praying somewhere. That was all she did these days. Her father was—where else?—working in his dry-cleaning shop. There was only the telephone, and if it rang she wouldn't answer it—not even if Barry called.

Barry was the real reason she wanted to stop thinking. If only he knew the truth about her. If only she could tell him, but every time she tried she felt as if she were going to choke.

She should have told him the night she met him, but how could she mention such terrible things in the middle of a church basement, with everyone drinking punch and eating cookies? What was she supposed to say when she was introduced to someone so good-looking?—"Hi, I'm a drunk, did you know that? And did you know I started to drink when I was thirteen? And I take pills and run around with a rough crowd? You wouldn't think it to look at me, but I could cut your heart out with a knife, or I could break your head wide open with a bicycle chain—I've been in fights like that. Once I almost killed a girl who was trying to steal my boyfriend. Yes, boyfriend. I've had lots of them. Would you like to be one?"

How she would have shocked him. No doubt about it, he was as respectable as they come. He was, in fact, the first respectable man who had ever attracted her. He belonged in this church. She didn't. She came only because she was curious about her mother, who had recently begun to pray and go to church. Ever since Liz could remember, her mother had been too drunk to go anywhere. She could only argue with Liz's father, usually about money. Now her mother didn't touch liquor. Good for her, Liz thought, but she wished her mother would leave her alone and stop preaching to her about being saved. Who wanted to be saved? Life was something to be spent, as fast as you could.

She should have ignored Barry that first night. She should have shaken hands and walked away—except that she liked the way he took her hand. His was warm and firm and—this was a word she rarely used—friendly. He was a few years older than she and quite a bit taller, and she liked standing next to him.

"You're new here?" he had said.

"Yes." That was when she should have told him terrible

things. There was nothing new about her. She was old, very, very old. Instead she said, "And you're not?" She could see that he liked it when she smiled.

"Been here all my life," he said, then he laughed. "I don't mean to sound so smug. It's just that I like it here. I hope you will, too."

She came back the next week, and something strange happened. She began to listen to the words of the prayers people were murmuring. They prayed for each other, for themselves, for friends and neighbors with problems and illnesses; they prayed about world conditions, both natural and political. And they uttered words of praise and thanksgiving to God for all his mercies, his love, his comfort.

She hadn't realized it would be so easy to pray, but listening to the voices around her, it seemed as if she could almost do it herself. There were no formal phrases to be memorized, no words she didn't understand. She felt as if she were listening to a conversation between two friends, except that she could hear only what one friend was saying to the other.

The urge to speak grew stronger. Finally, she clasped her hands tightly and bowed her head. She closed her eyes, and there in the almost-darkness she was alone. But not alone—someone was there. She sensed a presence, and suddenly she had to cry out to keep the presence with her. She needed it. "God!" she whispered in a hoarse voice choked with unexpected tears. That one word was the sole content of her prayer, but with it she had made contact. *God was there!*

How can I ever be the same? she wondered as she lay awake in her bed that night. Now she understood what had happened to her mother and why she could give up drinking. In the presence of God, Liz had looked back at herself, almost as if she had stepped outside her being. She did not like what she saw. It sickened her. It would sicken God too, but she would not let him see her like that. She would be different.

So Liz was different, not only for God, but for Barry, too. She decided that she didn't have to stop drinking altogether; she could just cut down. She would stay away from her old friends because they were always getting into trouble, and she would make new friends. She did not touch a drop of liquor all day before a prayer meeting; she did not dare let Barry smell alcohol on her breath as they lingered outside the church, talking.

Eventually Barry began to call for her and drive her home after the meetings. And then they began to see each other several times a week. That was when Liz decided not to drink at all. She could see what was happening to her and Barry: they were falling in love. She should have been happy, but part of her was frightened. What would happen if Barry knew the truth about her? Would he look at her with the same disgust she had for herself? Even if no one told him about her, how could she be sure she would not return to the old ways? The temptations were still there. She could sense them just below the surface of her awareness.

The more she thought about her deception, the more desperate she became. She wanted a drink to calm her nerves. Oh, how she wanted a drink! She was on her way to the bottle hidden in the basement when her Uncle Lou stopped in and gave her that little blue box.

Dear Uncle Lou. He was her father's brother, and ever since Liz had been a child he had tried to make up for all the time Liz's father was away from home. He had a family of his own, yet he always seemed to have time for Liz. He was the one—the only one—who came to see her when she was locked away in those mental wards. He would bring her candy and fruit and flowers, and he would sit by the hour watching her stare into space, all the while talking about the ordinary little events of life outside the hospital. Sometimes she cried, and he cried, too, but he would always walk away for a few minutes until he regained control of himself. He did not think it was manly for him to cry, but Liz thought it was the most loving thing anyone had ever done for her.

Yes, dear Uncle Lou who had brought her this beautiful pin. How had he known? She had told no one about the change that had come into her life. She kept her prayers to herself. Did they show?

Anyway, it was too late. She had already tried God, and it had worked, for a while. But now, God was just too painful.

She locked the door of her bedroom and put the bottle and a glass on the night table beside her bed. She stood there looking at them a moment, and then she rummaged through her bureau drawers, pulling out little packages of pills and pot she had hidden there. As long as she was about to go over the edge, she would do it in style.

"Go 'way!" she grunted when they started banging on her bedroom door. All those voices, all that noise—why didn't they leave her alone?

She lay motionless on her bed, listening to the sounds of someone picking at the lock with a knife. The room was dark, and when the door opened, a wave of light hit her eyes, and she shielded them with her hands.

Barry was there, close to her, bending over her. He looked as if he were in pain. He looked terrible. So did her mother, standing just behind him. Liz thought she heard her Uncle Lou's voice, but she didn't see him.

She felt Barry's arms go under her, and he lifted her up into a sitting position. Why was he shouting at her? What was he saying? He was shaking her by the shoulders, and her head was going to snap off. She took a deep breath and pulled herself free of him. "Stop it!" she screamed. "Get out of here and leave me alone!"

He was staring at the night table, at the bottle and the glass and the twisted pieces of paper. Well, he knew. It was all over. No more suspense. He knew.

"Yours?" he said, pointing.

She nodded her head.

Suddenly he bent down and scooped up the glass and the bottle and the papers and left the room. They could hear him in the kitchen, smashing the bottle in the sink. *Why?* she thought. *The bottle is empty.*

Then he came back and began to take her room apart, drawer by drawer. Her Uncle Lou helped him. They even took the pictures down from the walls and examined the frames.

She was surprised. They found capsules in some envelopes she did not remember hiding away. She must have been drunk when she hid them.

Barry gathered them in his hands. "Here," he said to Lou, "take them into the kitchen."

Liz's mother sank down on the bed and began to sob. "She'll only get more," she whimpered. "She always gets more."

Barry took Liz's arm and pulled her to her feet roughly. "Come with me," he said, tightening his grip. Her legs were unsteady, and she stumbled along behind him, hating him. *Why didn't he just go?* Let it be over.

"Now you stand here and watch," he said angrily as he pulled her to the kitchen sink and turned on the water. He removed the drain. The he held up one of the little white envelopes he had found in her room. As she watched, weaving slightly back and forth, he poured the capsules into the drain. They disappeared immediately, and the water swirled after them.

Over and over he did it, each time making sure that she saw the envelope and watched him empty it. If she tried to turn away he pulled her back. She was a little afraid of him.

The last to go were two marijuana cigarettes. He crushed them, shredded them into the water, rinsed every particle down the drain, and turned off the tap.

He looked at her and put his hands on her shoulders. All his anger was gone now, and his face was haggard. He started to speak several times and changed his mind. Finally he said, "Liz, I love you very much," and could say no more. He held her close to him, as if she were something precious. How could he possibly feel that way about her now? She was despicable.

"I can't lose you," he said.

Lou saw that she was still wearing the pendant. He remembered that he had seen the box in her room, and he went to get it. He took it with him into the kitchen and picked up the phone. He dialed Information and asked the operator, "Can you give me the number for The Walter Hoving Home in Garrison, New York, please?"

CHAPTER 19

In the first month after the "Try God" pins went on sale, 4,715 were sold. That meant over $34,000 for the Home. It was only the beginning. Hoving ran the ad again, this time in *The New Yorker* magazine as well as *The New York Times*. The response was the same—wonderful.

On New Year's Day Billy Graham invited his viewers to write in for a pin. He received 102,000 requests. (As of March 1977 the Graham organization had distributed 553,000 pins.)

John Benton found that at last he had time to think about other problems, and the Home had plenty of them. The most pressing one was "the eight-month dropout rate."

For the past few years the staff had been aware of a restlessness in some of the girls after they had spent about seven months at the Home. The passes didn't seem to help. The girls began to lose their enthusiasm and became easily irritated. After eight months—almost to the day—the staff knew that some of the girls would leave. They weren't ready to go home, and they knew it. Still they left. Elsie Benton packed each girl a box lunch to take with her and included a note telling her that the staff and the other girls loved her very much and hoped she would come back. They would pray for her, Elsie said.

The staff tried to keep in touch with the dropouts, but eventually they disappeared. Whenever they did get news, it was bad.

A few of the girls came back, but the way was not made easy for them. The Bentons had learned a lot about love. It had to be firm, it had to give a girl something to stand on. So now, when a girl came back after dropping out, she was put on "restriction" for two months: she could not communicate with the outside world in any way, not by telephone or letter or visits; nor could she receive communications from the outside world.

Elsie Benton felt like the meanest person in the world the first time she told a dropout she would be restricted. But even though most of the girls complained about it, they actually felt relieved. They wanted to be cut off from their former environment, yet they were unable to break the ties. They were grateful that someone else did it for them.

"It gives me a feeling of peace," one of the girls told Elsie, which prompted Elsie to decide that if a girl dropped out more than once, she should be put on a longer restriction each time she came back.

But the eight-month dropout rate was a mystery. It came such a short time after a girl began to feel confident in her new life. Why *then*?

The staff talked it over one day at a meeting and came up with the answer: boredom. During the first seven months at the Home a girl's life was filled with challenges, so that each time she met one of them she was excited. Every day became an adventure to her. Gradually there were fewer challenges and the adventure wore off.

"But that's part of growing up," one of the staff said. "Life isn't one big drumbeat after another."

"Let's face it," John Benton said, "even after eight

months at the Home, these girls are very immature. They still need a sense of achievement to get them through the next four months, but we can't simply manufacture challenges. They have to be real, the kind they're going to face once they get out in the world again." He rubbed his chin with his hand. "Boredom itself is a real challenge, so maybe we have to teach our girls how to deal with it." He waved his hand toward the window. "There's plenty of boredom in the world!"

The staff agreed. Then they came up with a plan. Each new girl would be assigned a "big sister," a girl who had been at the Home seven months or more. A girl wasn't likely to feel bored if she felt responsible for someone else. Helping another girl would also give her an awareness of her own increasing strength. The plan was put into effect immediately.

"My mother should see me now!" Liz was on her knees, a bucket of soapy water by her side and a wet cloth in her hand. She was washing the baseboards in one of the first-floor corridors of the main house. She sat back on her heels and wiped her forehead. "She never could get me to do anything around the house."

Sue was standing on tiptoes a few feet away, reaching up as high as she could to wash the woodwork around a closet door. She glanced down at Liz. "You're not doing much around here, either," she said, laughing. "You take a break every five minutes."

"Give me time, big sister, give me time. I don't have your willpower—don't you remember what it's like to want just one little drink?"

Sue nodded and kept on with her work.

"And just one little cigarette?" Liz said.

Sue came over to dip her cloth in the bucket. "Sure I

do," she said. "But I think you helped me to remember. And I'm glad."

"*I* helped *you?* I thought it was supposed to be the other way around."

"It works both ways," Sue said. "After you've been here for a while you forget what you were like when you came. In a way, that's good, because who wants to think about things like that? But in another way, it makes you self-centered. You keep thinking about how wonderful your own life is—and you forget that other people need the same kind of help you got." She patted Liz on the shoulder. "So thanks, little sister."

All the housework in the Home is done by the girls. So is the cooking. Classes are planned for the mornings, so that the girls can do their chores in the afternoons. They also keep up the grounds. The Home is immaculate.

"I think it's a miracle—the way you girls manage in that kitchen," John Benton said to the girls at his table one day at lunch. They laughed.

"Seriously," Benton protested, "it's not easy to learn how to cook for so many people. And a lot of you girls never learned how to cook at all."

"We still can't!" said a girl at another table.

"Brother B, if you could see what goes on in there most of the time, you wouldn't call it a miracle," the girl on his right said. "My first week on kitchen duty, I spent sitting in the middle of the floor, crying. I thought I'd never be able to do anything right."

Benton grinned. "Exactly. Yet we always get a great meal. So you see what I mean by a miracle?"

Liz was glad she wasn't working in the kitchen this week. She had hardly eaten for the first few days after her Uncle Lou drove her up to the Home, but in the weeks after that she had stuffed herself, going back for seconds, even thirds. The other girls told her it was perfectly normal, that going off liquor and cigarettes would increase her appetite. One of these days she would have to go on a diet. Elsie Benton was already nudging her in that direction.

Liz shifted her position and went back to work. Yes, her mother should see her now. And soon she would. At least that was Liz's hope.

When a girl had spent six weeks at the Home she was interviewed by several staff members to determine whether she sincerely wanted to give her life to Christ. If she didn't, she would have to leave—although she could come back and try again. But if the staff felt that a girl truly wanted to let Christ make her over into a new person, the girl was officially "accepted" into the Home at a Sunday service to which her family and friends were invited.

Liz was surprised by the depth of her longing to see her mother, her Uncle Lou—and especially Barry. She could only barely remember the last time she had seen Barry, that night at her house when he had tried to wash her past down the drain. He knew, and yet he loved her. She was afraid to believe it.

She wanted to be accepted into the Home. Would they believe that she was sincere? *Was* she sincere? She honestly didn't know.

Her relationship with God had changed, she realized that. She had never been able to hide anything from him, after all, and she felt that she was forgiven. But how long would that feeling last?

"Sue?"

"Uh-huh?"

"Sue—how do you know when you're doing the right thing?"

Sue put down her cloth and thought a moment. "That's not easy to answer, Liz. I mean, I probably could explain it better in a couple of weeks."

"Why then?"

"Because after you get into the habit of letting Christ make your decisions, you know whether something is right or wrong."

"But *how* do you feel? *What* do you feel? I never feel anything—I just have to take a guess."

Sue came and sat down on the floor beside her, leaning back against the wall and hugging her knees with her arms. "I used to be that way, too. I told myself I had given my life to Christ, but I was still trying to make my own decisions. When you let him do it, you won't be confused by right and wrong." She laughed. "Now, don't think you won't ever do anything wrong again," she said, "because you're still human. You'll make mistakes, but Christ won't let you get away with them. He'll point them out to you—you'll feel—well, we call it 'convicted.'"

"Sounds terrible," Liz said, frowning.

"No, it really isn't. It's wonderful, because once you know you've done something wrong you can learn from it. And you're forgiven every time, if you're really sorry about it."

Liz stood up abruptly. "Well, I don't want to feel convicted," she said, throwing her cloth into the bucket.

Sue wiped up the water that splashed over onto the carpet. "You're the one who said it—Give yourself time."

Suddenly, out of a deep sleep, Liz sat straight up in her bed. Her heart was beating so loudly she could not hear another sound, and she was listening very carefully.

The room was dark except for a little moonlight coming through the windowshade. Gradually her heartbeat slowed and she heard the sounds of her roommates breathing softly, regularly.

Then she realized that it wasn't a sound that had awakened her. She had smelled something, something she recognized from another time and place. Glue! Someone was sniffing glue right in her room. The stabbing scent was still there.

As her eyes became accustomed to the room, she could make out the forms on the double bunk beds across the room. Both girls were facing her, sound asleep.

Silently she slid out of her bed, gripped the bedpost, put one foot on her mattress, and hoisted herself up to look at the bunk above hers. Debbie had the covers pulled up over her head, but the smell of glue was stronger.

Liz pulled the covers away from Debbie's face. "You're crazy!" she whispered.

"Sh-h-h!" Debbie sat up and pulled the blankets around her. She giggled foolishly. "Want some?" she said.

"Where did you get that?" Liz said. But she knew. Debbie must have stolen it from the art supplies.

"Have some," Debbie said, holding out her hand. "You need something to help you get through the day—you know that," she taunted.

Liz drew back, afraid. "Not that. Do me a favor—don't use that around me."

Debbie laughed softly and curled up on her bed, pulling the blankets up around her head. The other girls were still asleep.

Liz sat on her bed. She couldn't sleep now. How could it happen? How could a girl who had been here as long as Debbie give it all up?

Liz wondered what she could do to protect herself. She knew that if she stayed in the same room with Debbie she would soon be sharing the glue with her. Liz wasn't strong enough to hold out. Maybe she could ask to be transferred to another room.

But what about the other girls? *All* the other girls? Debbie was destroying the Home just as surely as if she had set fire to it. If one girl could break the rules, why couldn't the rest of them?

She could not betray Debbie. That was out of the question. In her world you didn't turn in a friend.

Wrong! She felt the word more than she heard it. She was wrong to protect Debbie. She would not help her by keeping her secret. Debbie needed to face the truth about herself.

Liz was miserable. The harder she tried to overcome the feeling of wrongness, the more powerful it became. She lay down and tried to sleep, but she couldn't. She tried to fill her mind with other thoughts—any thoughts, even the words to a song—but nothing else seemed to exist.

And then she remembered her conversation with Sue a few days earlier. No need to ask—now she knew how it felt to be convicted.

She turned on her side and lay very still. She closed her eyes. "Thank you, Lord!" As she prayed for Debbie, as she asked Christ what she must do, her tears began to fall onto her pillow. For the first time she began to feel that there was hope for her future. She did not have to rely on herself; she could trust God.

Liz waited by the front door of the dormitory, watching for Sue to come down the stairs on her way to lunch. When she saw Sue, she waved. Sue did not wave back, nor did she smile.

"I'm sorry about Debbie," Liz said. There had been a hearing early in the morning. Liz had been asked to confront Debbie with what she had seen the night before. Debbie had offered no excuses, but she pleaded for forgiveness.

"You know you have that," Elsie Benton said. "But you'll have to leave the Home."

Liz was shocked. She hadn't expected such severe discipline.

"If I had known," she tried to explain to Sue, "I don't know if I would have told anybody."

"You *had* to do it, Liz—I'm glad you did. I just feel so sick about Debbie. How could she do it?"

"What'll happen to her now?"

"Who knows? Just pray that she tries to come back."

"Do they *have* to send her away? It was just one mistake."

"Look, Liz, we all started out making that one little mistake. You know where it leads."

Sue started to walk toward the house. Liz caught up with her. Yes, Debbie had to leave, Liz realized that now. She would have been afraid to let her stay.

After a few months the staff decided that the mystery of the eight-month dropout rate had been solved. Being a big sister gave a girl an opportunity to use resources she didn't know she had. Once she realized she could help another girl, she began to grow up. Giving attention rather than demanding it became a new kind of adventure.

"Too bad we didn't think of it in time to help Debbie," John Benton said. He never got used to the pain he felt each time a girl dropped out.

"Well, at least she didn't take Sue with her. I think Sue's going to make it," Elsie said.

"So do I."

CHAPTER 20

Walter Hoving was annoyed. An executive of the American Civil Liberties Union had written him, asking for documented proof of the 90 per cent cure rate mentioned in the Tiffany ad. The letter expressed serious doubt that such a claim could be proved.

Hoving sent the letter to John Benton, who replied and included a copy of *The Hoving Home Highlighter*, a monthly newsletter.

Another letter came back: ". . . These publications do not provide responses to any of the questions raised in my letter. . . . They do suggest, however, that there is a very serious misstatement in the advertisements Tiffany's has been placing in *The New Yorker* and *The New York Times*. Those advertisements say that, after a year's treatment, over 90 per cent of drug-addicted girls in The Walter Hoving Home, Inc., are permanently cured. The newsletter you sent me says something very different. It says: 'Nine out of the ten girls who have completed the full one-year program remain free from their old way of life.' And, in describing the old way of life from which the girls have been freed, it says they 'have been involved in drug addiction, alcoholism, deliquency, and other serious problems.'

"If it exists, I would still like to see support for the claim made in Tiffany's advertisements. Everything I know about drug addiction tells me it is highly improbable that this claim can be supported. I hope you can do better in persuading me that there is some basis for Tiffany's advertising."

Hoving knew John Benton could handle it, but he wanted to add something.

"Yes, I think you are right," he wrote. "Everything you know about drug addiction tells you it is highly improbable that this claim can be supported. But I believe you have apparently only been exposed to government-funded or partially government-funded drug abuse centers as well as some others. Their cure rate runs between 10 per cent and 18 per cent. . . .

"You see, our operation is run on a different principle. It's based on the fact that you have to change the person before you attack the problem. These girls are changed by accepting Jesus Christ into their lives—hence the cure rate. As a matter of fact, the government funded a research project for one of the Teen Challenge operations for boys. They spent $175,000 and, although not yet completed, it shows a cure rate of approximately 70 per cent. They are astonished, to say the least.

"The statement 'have been involved in drug addiction, alcoholism, delinquency, and other serious problems' does not mean that girls are suffering from all four. Now, if you'd like to make an independent study of this operation, we'd be glad to cooperate with any outside outfit—but, of course, we would expect you to fund it. Such a study, however, will find that our cure rate is over 90 per cent."

That should end it, he thought. But by return mail came the request:

"Please let me know where I might get a copy of any report on this research project or any person I can contact to find out about it."

With a sigh, Hoving asked Anne Balsan to get his copy of a recent Teen Challenge report on a government study. He dictated a short note to accompany it: "Here's a preliminary finding showing an 84 per cent cure rate for one of our other operations."

That did end the matter.

Elsie Benton barely recognized the voice. It was hoarse, and the connection was poor. "Can you speak a little louder?" Elsie said.

"I said, 'It's Sandy McKay.'" She was angry, but then, Sandy always was angry.

"I thought so, but you sound different. How are you, Sandy?"

"Rotten. I want to come back."

"Do you mean it?"

"Yes!"

Elsie wasn't taking any chances. "Give me your address. I'll ask someone from Teen Challenge to come and get you."

"There's someone with me," Sandy said. "A friend of mine named Carol. We're in bad shape."

"Sandy, I'd better tell you before you come—you'll have to be restricted for two months because you didn't stay last time. That means no letters, no phone calls or visits—not from anyone."

"I don't care. My daughter's the only one I want to talk to."

"Not even her, Sandy. No one. You'll be completely cut off."

"You people must eat nails for breakfast," Sandy muttered. In the silence that followed, Elsie prayed. "Okay," Sandy said. "It's probably better that way. Send your friends over."

CHAPTER 21

It would be different this time, Sandy knew. This time she would stay at the Home. She was desperate enough.

As she walked the half block from the telephone booth to the dingy room where Carol was waiting, she looked around for the last time. She never wanted to come back, at least not to this part of the city.

She had lived in the streets for six months. Sometimes she rented a room, sometimes only a bed in a room filled with girls like her, each of them terrified of the harm that might come to her from the others. And there were times when she slept in a hallway or on a fire escape or in a car whose owner had neglected to lock the doors.

She was better off than most of the other girls on the street. She wasn't a prostitute. Usually she could find a job in a hospital because she had experience as a nurse's aid. But the money wasn't much, and she had expensive habits. Between liquor and pills, she was always broke. So to make up the difference, she stole.

She had been stealing since she was a child, and to her it was a game. She had no moral misgivings about it, partly because she had never been told it was wrong to steal, and partly because she had contempt for the way storekeepers displayed their wares—if they were foolish enough to give her access to them, they deserved to be robbed. At times she convinced herself that she was teaching them a lesson.

Carol wasn't as lucky. She had no particular talents, which only increased Sandy's feeling of responsibility toward her. From the first time she saw Carol, when Carol was brought into the hospital emergency room where Sandy was working the twelve to eight shift, Sandy felt that she had to watch over her. Carol had almost died from an overdose of heroin, and her arms were full of needle marks, but she survived. And when she was ready to be discharged, she looked so pale and weak that Sandy could not let her go off by herself. Someone had to take care of her. So Sandy offered to let her share her room and her food and her pills and her liquor. But no heroin. Sandy knew where to draw the line.

Sandy didn't understand this softhearted part of her personality. It was out of place in her life. It drew her to work in sickrooms and made her astonishingly gentle with the handicapped. But it also made her sympathetic toward someone like Carol, and that was a mistake. Now Sandy had to steal for two, because Carol was totally incapable of bringing in any money—unless she did the very things that had almost cost her her life.

Once Carol had been a beautiful girl, which led her to believe she didn't have to be anything else. Men gave her whatever she needed until finally they gave her too much. Someone introduced her to heroin.

In time the long, dark brown hair lost its shine. The clear skin became a sickly gray in color, and there were ugly sores that didn't heal. Carol's eyes were swollen and watery, and she sniffled most of the time. Carol wasn't beautiful anymore, and the men were gone.

She did whatever she could. If she could stay away

from drugs for a few days, she looked presentable enough to get a job as a waitress in one of the cheaper nightclubs. Then, because she didn't think she had any choice, she let one of the club managers talk her into becoming a stripper. As long as she could stay high, she didn't care what she did.

In the clubs drugs were plentiful, and Carol became a greedy consumer. She was told she was getting too ugly to be a stripper; she tossed her hair, which was now several shades of blond and dark at the roots. Let them fire her—there was always prostitution.

Carol didn't intend to take an overdose. It was an accident. But she was badly shaken by it. For the first time she wanted to break the drug habit, and the best way to do it was to stay away from the clubs. Sandy was helping her to do that.

They were an unfortunate combination. In order to keep Carol off heroin, Sandy gave her anything else she could buy or steal. And to keep her company, Sandy herself doubled her consumption of liquor and pills. She lost track of time and was late for work so often that she was fired. She could get another job, she told herself, but when she looked at herself in a mirror, she knew it wasn't true. She looked almost as bad as Carol. She was emaciated because she was too drugged to steal food for the two of them. She would leave their room and get as far as the front door of the building, where she sat down on the steps and hung her head drowsily. She would sit there for hours and go back to the room empty-handed.

"We've got to do something," she said to Carol.

Carol nodded slowly.

"You've got to help me straighten out," Sandy began, and shook her head. "No, you can't—you can't do anything."

"Yes, I can," Carol said softly. "It's time I went back to work."

"Oh, no—not the clubs. You'll be dead in a week."

"I won't live any longer this way, Sandy. We're starving to death."

They sat quietly, staring at each other. Carol was right, Sandy decided, they were dying, and there wasn't anything they could do about it. They were too weak, too sick, too exhausted. They needed help. That was when Sandy left the room and walked down the street to the telephone booth.

When she came back, she told Carol to pack up her clothes and get ready to take a little ride. "But first, we're going to make sure we don't know where we're going," she said. She had spent her last few dollars on some cheap wine, and somewhere in the room she had a few more pills she was saving for a special occasion.

Poor Carol. Drunk as she was, she was confused by the prayers of the two young men from Teen Challenge. Even Sandy, who knew what to expect, thought they were overdoing it. One sat in the back seat of the car between her and Carol and the other drove, and they didn't stop praying. They had never seen the two girls before, yet they were asking God to do all kinds of wonderful things for them.

Oh, well, Sandy reminded herself, *it was better than being on the streets.* This time she was going to be patient with these people—because she just didn't know where else to go.

CHAPTER 22

Many times during the next three days Sandy forced herself to remember exactly what it was like in the streets. That was the only way she could get through the abrupt withdrawal from alcohol and drugs.

She could not eat. She had pains in her stomach and in her head. She felt dizzy and she was weak from vomiting. If only she could have a cigarette! Just one cigarette! All she got were prayers and soft words and arms that steadied her as she paced her room until she was ready to sleep from exhaustion.

But the sickness passed. On the fourth day she woke up hungry and knew she was going to be all right. She remembered where she was and why she had come. And Carol—she remembered Carol. They had not seen each other since the night they arrived at the Home.

When Sandy walked into the dining room, Elsie Benton waved her over to a table.

"I knew you could do it, Sandy," Elsie said, squeezing her hand. "This time you let the Lord help you."

Sandy smiled. "I still want a cigarette," she said.

"Of course you do. But you'll get over it. Have some breakfast instead."

Sandy had never been so hungry in her life. She went

back to the kitchen twice after her first helping of pancakes and sausages. The coffee tasted especially good.

"How about some milk?" Elsie Benton said.

"I never drink milk."

"Then it's time you started." Elsie put a glass of milk in front of her. Stubbornly, Sandy refused to look at it.

"Where's Carol?" Sandy asked.

"I think she went down to the rose garden," Elsie said, turning toward the windows behind her. "Down there," she said pointing. They were sitting in the new section of the dining room, a long, narrow room enclosed on three sides with windows. The view was lovely, especially on such a sunny day.

"Carol isn't doing too well," Elsie said, as Sandy gathered up her dishes.

"Is she still sick?"

"In a way. She's over the physical part of it, but there's more to it than that." Elsie reached for the glass of milk and poured some into her coffee. "Sandy—how much did you tell her about the Home?"

"Not much. There wasn't time."

"Well—I think we were a bit of a shock to her."

"I'll talk to her," Sandy said. They didn't know how to handle Carol, that's all.

The spring sunshine was warm. Sandy took off her sweater as she walked down the hill toward the rose garden so that she could enjoy the sun on her arms. It was good to be in the country. The smell of it was delicious. In fact, Sandy realized, all her senses were coming back to life, which made her feel more comfortable in the world. A branch of buds and leaves would have been something to push out of the way; now it was something to touch, to smell, to look back at.

Carol was sitting on the grass at the bottom of the hill where the rose bushes were beginning to show color. Her face was turned up to the sun, her eyes closed tightly against the brightness.

She must have seen Sandy coming. "I've been waiting for you," she said, without opening her eyes.

Sandy sat down opposite her, her back to the sun. "Long?"

"Four days."

Sandy laughed.

"I mean it, Sandy," Carol said. "I wanted to leave that first night—but I didn't want to go without you."

Sandy felt a wave of nausea. Suddenly she was afraid. "How do you feel?" she said.

"I'm okay—but this is some crazy place! How did you find out about it?"

"It's a long story. I'll tell you sometime."

"All this religion—I can't take it. I don't want to spend my life praying."

Sandy tried to laugh. "You don't have to. They manage to do some other things, too."

Carol stood up and brushed some pieces of grass off her jeans. "Not me," she said. "Sandy, I'm all packed—I never *un*packed. There's a train from Garrison to New York—and they'll drive us to the station."

Sandy looked down at the grass and ran her hand over it lightly.

"Sandy?" Carol said. "Are you coming?" She shielded her eyes with her hand.

"No."

"Okay. I'll miss you."

Sandy looked up at her. Carol's eyes were wet, and she blinked back her tears. "What will you do?"

Carol shook her hair. "Go back to work," she said, and

Sandy knew what that meant. "It's a living," Carol said apologetically.

"Carol, neither one of us knows what the word 'living' really means because we've never done it. We've been dying from the minute we were born. That's why I came here—I want to find out what it's like to live. And that's why I won't go with you."

Carol turned and started up the hill. Then she stopped. "Ask them where my room is," she said. "I'll leave you a couple of blouses and a pair of jeans." She put her hand up to her eyes again. "You'll need them more than I will." She tried to smile, but couldn't.

Watching her walk up the hill, Sandy thought that Carol looked as helpless as she did the night they brought her into the hospital on a stretcher. Who would take care of her now?

Sandy forced herself to sit there in the rose garden until Carol was completely out of sight. "I hope you know what you're doing, God," she muttered, "because I don't!"

CHAPTER 23

For the first time in her life Sandy memorized something. It was a simple Bible verse—"For with God nothing shall be impossible" (Lk. 1:37)—but it took her a long time to repeat it correctly. Her mind was not accustomed to discipline.

When she could say the verse without halting, she began to pay attention to its meaning. She thought God must have intended the words especially for her, and it was no coincidence that it was the first assignment in the first class she attended. *Only* with God was anything possible for Sandy.

She could hardly believe the changes that were taking place in her. Occasionally another girl irritated her to the point where she wanted to throw something at her, but she was learning what to do with her anger. She prayed about it—excitedly, vehemently, letting God know exactly how she felt and the terrible things she wanted to do. Putting words around the turbulence inside her was a relief. It allowed her to be quiet for a while, to listen for the message she now knew would come—*Go and talk to the girl.*

Amazingly, she could do it. She could approach a girl she had wanted to choke and ask her to sit down and talk over their differences. Getting grudges out in the open made all the difference, and the two girls usually became friends. And Sandy, no longer feeling as if she were about to explode, could pay attention to other areas of her life.

Her language, for example. She knew and had used every street word in the book, without realizing it. One day, in a Personal Improvement class, the girls were asked to write down all the street words they could remember. Pens moved rapidly across the sheets of paper, covering them with columns of profanity. Looking around her, Sandy felt at home. But long after the other girls were finished, Sandy was still writing. She was embarrassed to find the class waiting for her.

"Too bad I can't get some kind of a degree in this," she joked, and the girls laughed, but inwardly Sandy was ashamed. She shouldn't have been, because the other girls also had been unaware of the quality of their language. "If I try to stop using all these words," one girl complained, "I won't be able to say anything."

Nobody asked them to change the way they spoke, but after they saw the words on paper they never were the same. They were different on the inside, and they wanted it to show. So without prompting from the instructors or counselors, the girls began to correct each other's choice of words.

Sandy worked harder than anyone. For a few days she was almost speechless from keeping a close guard on her mouth, but finally she had to admit that she was beginning to sound like a lady. She also was beginning to sit, walk, and stand like a lady, thanks to a few more classes in Personal Improvement. Wait until her daughter saw her. . . .

The lack of communication with her daughter was the only part of her two months' restriction that bothered

Sandy. She was glad Carol could not reach her, because she wasn't sure she could resist a plea for help. And she was happy to be away from any source of pills, because she still could not say "No" to them. She did not even want to remember that such things existed, at least for a while. She needed time to sort out her problems and decide which ones she was strong enough to approach.

The most difficult problem was going to be her daughter. Hope was eight years old now and very happy with her foster parents. They were good people who loved the child and wanted to adopt her, yet they respected Sandy's feelings. But it was difficult for Hope to grow up with two mothers, especially when one of them was little more than a voice on the telephone.

Hope didn't have the same difficulty with fathers; as far as she knew, she only had one, her foster father, whom she adored. She had never seen her real father. Joe, Sandy's husband, might be dead, for all Sandy knew, except that every once in a while an FBI agent tracked her down to ask her if she knew where Joe was. He was still wanted on several forgery charges. "You'll know before I do," Sandy always said.

Whenever she allowed herself to think about her problems she became depressed. It would be a long time before she was able to do anything about them. Maybe never. But then, she reminded herself, ". . . with God nothing shall be impossible," and almost immediately a sense of peace returned to her.

"Ow-w-w!"

Sandy dropped to her knees and gripped her right forefinger in her left hand. She clenched her teeth as the tears came to her eyes.

She had been playing baseball with a few other girls,

and it was her turn at bat. She stood in a slight crouch, holding the bat up against her right shoulder and doing her best to unnerve the pitcher with a fierce scowl. As the ball came at her she swung as hard as she could and only at the last moment realized that she was swinging too high. The ball smashed into her finger, knocking the bat from her hands.

"I'm all right," she said to the circle of girls who stood around her. Liz knelt down and pulled Sandy's left hand away from the injured finger.

"Can you move it?" Liz said.

"Who wants to!" Sandy snapped. The pain was getting worse.

"Try wiggling it," Liz insisted. Sandy couldn't. "I think it's broken," Liz said. "Let's go find Mom B."

Up at the house Elsie Benton agreed with Liz that Sandy needed a doctor. "I'll drive you to the hospital," she said, and put her arm around Sandy as she led her out to the station wagon. The pain was so bad that Sandy could not object.

"No bandage?" Sandy asked the resident who examined her finger.

"No—we don't do that anymore with broken fingers. Not unless there are complications."

"You mean I just walk around with it like this?" she said, holding up her finger.

"I wouldn't hold it up in the air if I were you," he said, smiling. "The X rays show a simple fracture. It will heal by itself if you don't use it for a while." He took a pen out of his pocket and reached for a pad on a small metal desk behind him.

"You'll have some pain for a few days," he said, as he began writing. "I'll prescribe something to make it bearable."

Sandy looked up anxiously at Elsie Benton. "Oh, no!"

she said, shaking her head rapidly. "That's something I don't need!"

The doctor was surprised. "The pain will get worse before it stops," he said.

"I don't care. Let it." She turned to Elsie Benton again. "You tell him why," she said. Between the pain and her fear, she felt sick.

"Sandy used to have a problem with pills," Elsie said. "Is there anything else we can do for the pain?"

"Aspirin?" the doctor said, looking at Sandy. She was very pale.

"Sandy, maybe you ought to take something," Elsie said. "I can see how much it hurts you."

When Sandy said nothing, the doctor went to a cabinet and took out a bottle of aspirin tablets. He put several of them into a small envelope and gave it to Sandy. "Would you like some water so you can take a few now?" he said.

Sandy shook her head. "I'll get some outside." She took the envelope and put it in her pocket.

Outside in the hallway they looked for a water fountain. When they found one Sandy took a long drink, and then refilled her paper cup. She looked at it a moment, then poured the water down the drain.

"Here," she said, handing the envelope of aspirin to Elsie, "take these and throw them away. Please."

"But it's only aspirin—"

"Mom B, I don't want to take *anything*. After the way I used to be, it's too big a risk."

"What about the pain, Sandy?" Elsie Benton said.

"Believe me, this is one pain I'm going to enjoy!" Sandy said.

Opposite the parking lot outside the main house a roomy two-story frame building had been turned into a garage, with a recreation room on the second floor. Sandy noticed that the garage had been cleared out and the tractors and landscaping equipment moved alongside the building.

"What's going on?" she asked Liz, who was opening a large carton.

"We're going to have a flea market," Liz said. "Want to help?"

"Sure. What do I do?"

"First you can help me sort these clothes we're going to sell. People donated so many, we can't use them all—but we can make a little money on them. It all helps."

"I thought we had plenty of money—from the 'Try God' pin." Sandy said.

"For now, sure. But not forever. We still have to take care of ourselves." She pointed to the corner where an ironing board was set up. "If you really want to help, you can press off some of these clothes." Then she saw Sandy's finger and remembered. "Not with that you can't," she said.

"You iron and I'll unpack," Sandy said. "I can do that with one hand."

Most of the clothes were beautiful and almost new. Holding up a child's coat with a fur-trimmed hood, Sandy tried to imagine how it would look on Hope. Perhaps she could buy the coat for her daughter—but she didn't know any of Hope's sizes. Sandy hadn't bought her anything to wear since she was an infant. The realization depressed her. How could she even consider the possibility of someday becoming a full-time mother to her daughter?

Liz noticed the change in Sandy's mood. "What's the matter?" she said. "Thinking abut the future?"

"How did you know?"

"We all do it—at first. The first few months I was here I

used to worry about all the problems that would be waiting for me when I went back home."

"How do you feel about them now?" Sandy asked.

Liz put the iron aside and began arranging a blouse on a hanger. "Well, I stopped worrying. And you will, too. But give yourself time."

"Why? I can't change what I've been—which was pretty bad."

"So was I, Sandy. Most of us were. If we had a contest to find out who made the biggest mess of her life, we'd all win some kind of prize."

"You know, it's hard for me to believe that about you. You look so happy and peaceful."

Liz laughed. "I am now. But I've been here awhile. I'm a different person. I told you about Barry—well, for the longest time I didn't want to see him when he came to visit me. I was uncomfortable knowing that he loved me, because I didn't understand how he could. I didn't understand how *anyone* could. I guess that was my trouble all along. I didn't think I was very lovable."

Sandy nodded. She knew the feeling.

"Sandy, one of these days you're going to realize that God loves you more than you could ever believe. And it's going to change you. It's going to make you like yourself. Then you'll be able to think about the future without worrying, because you'll know that Jesus will be there to help you."

"Liz, does Barry want you to marry him?"

"Yes."

"Are you going to?"

"Yes. But I wouldn't have said that a few months ago. I didn't think I was good enough for him then."

"What about now?"

"Well—I'm good enough for God," Liz said.

A few days earlier, Liz had returned from a week at home. At the last minute she had tried to cancel the trip, but Elsie Benton had talked her into it again.

"You can't cross your parents out of your life," Elsie had said. "You have to try to get along with them—give them a chance."

"My father hates me, Mom B—he always has. He never wanted me."

"I'm not asking you to forget that, Liz. But give yourself a chance to look at your father through different eyes. You've got Jesus in your heart now, honey, and everything is going to look different to you. When nobody loves you, when you're all alone, you can't take rejection. I know. But when you know how much God loves you, you can see past the hurt and maybe figure out why a person behaves that way. Usually it doesn't have anything to do with you—it's the other person who's in trouble."

For a while, then, Liz looked forward to going home. She wanted to see her mother and Barry and her Uncle Lou, and—yes, even her father. But sitting in Barry's car outside her house, she was afraid. She didn't want to go in. She didn't want to relive the events that made her try to destroy herself.

Barry took her hand. "Liz, I'm right here with you," he said.

"Not yet," she said. "Can't we drive around for a while?"

"No. They're waiting for us."

She let him lead her to the front door, and her mother met her on the steps. Liz held her close. Over her mother's shoulder she saw her Uncle Lou, smiling and waiting to give her one of his bear hugs. He was wearing a "Try God" pin in his lapel. Liz touched the thin gold chain around her neck and held out the pendant. "Thanks again, Uncle Lou," she said.

In the living room she saw her father standing at the front window. He must have been watching her from there. And he was crying. He stood motionless, looking at her, his arms at his sides.

Suddenly she sensed the pain that was in the man, the fear that had always been in control of him. He was not a very talented person, but he had worked hard to give his family what he considered the best things in life. He gave them things in place of himself, because he didn't think he was worth giving. That was why he kept his distance. Oh, how well she understood exactly how he must have felt.

"Daddy!" she said. She ran to him and hugged him as hard as she could. Her tears fell on his shoulder as his arms went around her. "It's all right now, Daddy!" she said. It's all right."

Sue was spending the weekend at the Home. Like many of the girls who graduated, she felt an occasional need to return. "I've met some wonderful people out there," she told Liz, "but this is where my family is."

Sue was attending a Bible college in the Midwest. When she finished she hoped to find a job helping other troubled girls. John Benton thought there might be a place for her in one of the Teen Challenge centers.

"Wonderful!" Sue said. "I'd really like to work with very young girls, if that's possible. You know—reach them before they get into serious trouble."

That gave John Benton an idea.

On Saturday the driveway was crowded with cars. It was sunny and cool, a perfect day for a flea market.

Sandy was proud of the way the garage looked. Clothes were hung on long racks along the sides, and in the middle, on tables covered with sheets, were lamps and dishes and other household items.

Most of the customers came from the Garrison area. A lot of them obviously came out of curiosity about the Home, but after they were there for a while they relaxed and enjoyed themselves. *Now, if only they'll buy,* Sandy thought. She was becoming impatient as she watched people pick up an item, say something nice about it, and put it back. "*You want it, you know you do!*" Sandy urged silently.

Liz had asked her to help sell the clothing, but Sandy couldn't bring herself to do it. "I haven't been to enough Personal Improvement classes yet," Sandy said. So she stayed on the sidelines—until finally she couldn't stand it any longer.

A tall, thin, serious-faced woman with iron-gray hair picked up the hooded coat that would have been just right for Hope. She held it up, and Sandy thought she saw a smile on the woman's face. She turned the coat over and over, and examined the lining and the collar. She started to put it down, then held it up again. She looked around, but the salesgirls were busy with other customers. The woman put the coat down and began to walk away.

Sandy caught up with her. "Excuse me, ma'am," she said, smiling as widely as she could. "I noticed you looking at that coat—Do you have a granddaughter about eight years old?"

The woman laughed. "Seven—how did you know?"

Sandy took her arm and gently guided her back toward the coat. "She must be a very pretty little girl, because that's a beautiful coat."

"Yes—it's nice."

Sandy held the coat in front of her, turning it from back to front. "Confidentially, this is the finest piece of clothing here. And it almost wasn't even here, because the minute I saw it I wanted it for my little girl. But she's eight, and this is too small. You can't get a coat like this for three times the price."

"That's true," the woman said thoughtfully. She bought the coat. And Sandy sold her a dress, some heavy woolen pants, and three sweaters along with it. When Sandy was counting out the change, the woman said, "You girls are awfully nice—you've been very helpful." She held out her hand, and Sandy shook it shyly. For the first time in her life, a stranger was offering her respect.

"Thank you, Lord," Sandy prayed silently as the woman walked away. "And now you'll have to excuse me while I go sell some things."

It was Sandy who brought the flea market to life. How she looked, how she spoke, what she had been meant nothing to her. The important thing was to put good merchandise in the hands of people who wanted it and at the same time make some money for the Home. She found something for everybody, and toward the end of the day, when the choice was dwindling down to a few picked-over items, she climbed up on a table and auctioned them off. People bought them for the sheer pleasure of seeing the happy smile on her face when they said "Yes."

"I didn't know you were so good at selling," Liz said as they counted the proceeds that night.

"Neither did I," Sandy said. "But nothing ever meant that much to me before, either." She was beginning to think that the future might not be so threatening, after all.

CHAPTER 24

Sue had brought John Benton sad news. Debbie was in prison, convicted of armed robbery.

"I went to see her," Sue told him, "and I'm going to keep writing to her." She didn't expect Debbie to answer her letters, at least not at first. Debbie was too ashamed, too frightened. "But she's the one who brought me here," Sue said, "and maybe someday I can bring her back."

If only they could reach these girls sooner, Benton thought. That must have been what was going through Sue's mind when she decided she wanted to work with younger people. "Get them before the trouble gets too big," Sue had said, and Benton agreed with her.

He got a lot of calls from ministers, social workers, and correctional officers who wanted to know if the Home could accommodate girls under seventeen. The answer had to be "No" because of the New York State law that forbade housing girls under seventeen with older girls. *Why does there have to be such a law?* Benton wondered.

No, he wasn't being fair. There was a good reason for the law, he was sure. Girls over seventeen could teach younger girls the wrong kind of things. As long as they were supervised, they would be all right, but in the leisure hours of the evening, there could be trouble. Nevertheless, if it weren't for that law . . .

The problem had been going around and around in his head, and then suddenly it was no longer a problem. Why not open another house for younger girls? They could sleep there and come to Garrison for classes. And if the Home didn't have enough money to buy such a house, it could rent one. The town of Cold Spring, only about five miles from the Home, would be a perfect location.

Elsie Benton was delighted with the idea. "How soon can we start looking at houses?" she said.

John laughed. "Wait a minute," he said, holding up his hand. "We can't just go out looking. It's not as easy as before. People know who we are, and they can pretty well figure out why we want a big house."

"You think there might be some opposition?"

"I don't want to sound pessimistic—but there still are a few people who don't want our girls as neighbors." He smiled at what he had said. "Listen to me," he said; "'our girls.'"

"Well, they are, in a way," Elsie said. "They're our family—every single one of them. And I think it's time for our family to grow."

Benton was right. There would be opposition to another home for girls.

"Not that these girls have done anything wrong since they've lived here," one person said. "It's just that we don't want to get too many of them."

But there also were people like Bill Roach, who had been uneasy when The Walter Hoving Home first came to Garrison. "I think these people are good neighbors," he said. "Not a single girl has ever caused the least bit of trouble. So why should anybody object to them?"

"You've got the right idea, John," Walter Hoving said. "Don't buy—rent. Later on, when people get used to the girls being there, you can buy the house."

Finding the right house at a reasonable price would be difficult. Moving in would be more of a problem. But, in his typically logical manner, Benton decided to take one step at a time. He wanted to give God every opportunity to let him know he was going in the right direction.

CHAPTER 25

At 10 A.M. on Thursday, June 17, 1976, The Walter Hoving Home Advisory Board met in the Tiffany conference room. Like most of the meetings during the past year, it was a happy occasion.

Since the "Try God" pins and pendants had been introduced seven months ago, 24,023 had been sold, bringing the total contribution to the Home to $190,211. And there was no sign of sales falling off. Whenever they decreased, Hoving ran the ad again and the figures rose. (As of March 1977 the total contribution had risen to $314,792.)

Forty-three girls were now at the Home. The staff was necessarily larger, and at last there were enough books and educational supplies to go around. The Bentons and their children had a small house of their own on the grounds.

Elsie smiled, hearing her husband report on the improvements. She had given up all thoughts of a house of her own. It had ceased to be important compared to the needs of the girls, and at times she wished she could compress her needs into the size of a broom closet. She thanked God for the room they had, and at the same time told him she would be just as grateful for less space. And now she had a house of her own.

The expanded dining room was the most important physical improvement that the "Try God" pin had made possible. Next, the driveway would be paved.

"When I think back to our first year, when we had only twelve girls, I can't believe we've come so far," Benton said. "But we don't want to get lazy. The 'Try God' pin put us on our feet, and now we want to help ourselves stay that way." He described plans for telephone canvassing and special fund-raising dinners.

"We just had a Walkathon, and you should have seen how many people walked twenty-five miles to raise money for the Home."

"I know," Walter Hoving said. "My secretary was one of them—and she had a cold. But she got pledges of nine hundred dollars."

"That's what I mean. We want to be ready—just in case the 'Try God' pin doesn't last forever."

"But it will, John, it will," Hoving said.

At the Board's September meeting, John Benton was able to report that thirty girls under sixteen could now be accommodated in a rented house in nearby Cold Spring.

"We already moved twelve girls in. They come to Garrison for classes. And we're giving them the equivalent of a high-school education. Of course, we have a bigger teaching staff, too."

The other Board members were pleased. "Do you have your certificate of occupancy yet?" someone asked.

"Not yet. There'll be a hearing."

When the meeting ended, Walter Hoving took John Benton aside. "What about this hearing, John?" he said. "Can we expect trouble?"

"I think so," Benton said, frowning. "If you'll pardon

the pun, Cold Spring isn't exactly warming to the idea. Frankly, I don't think we'll be able to stay there."

"Well, we've been through this before, John. But we can expect some help, too."

Benton's face relaxed into a smile. "Yes—and I already got some," he said. He reached into his jacket pocket for a small pad and a pen. Holding the pad in the palm of his hand, he began to sketch rough lines on a blank sheet. "Last night I got an idea," he said as he drew. "If we were to shift some things around, we could fit the new girls into one building by themselves. It'll be a bit crowded, but—"

"That's wonderful!" Hoving said. "Maybe we were in too much of a hurry. Maybe the good Lord is telling us we have to fill up the space we have before he gives us more. And he will, John, he will."

"I have the same feeling," Benton said. "In fact, I'm counting on it."

BROADMAN